Sidney Dyer

Black diamonds

Or, The curiosities of Coal

Sidney Dyer

Black diamonds
Or, The curiosities of Coal

ISBN/EAN: 9783743327214

Manufactured in Europe, USA, Canada, Australia, Japa

Cover: Foto ©ninafisch / pixelio.de

Manufactured and distributed by brebook publishing software (www.brebook.com)

Sidney Dyer

Black diamonds

Black Diamonds

or the

Curiosities

of

Coal

BLACK DIAMONDS;

OR, THE

CURIOSITIES OF COAL.

BY

Rev. SIDNEY DYER, A. M.,

AUTHOR OF "GREAT WONDERS IN LITTLE THINGS," "HOME AND ABROAD," ETC.

PHILADELPHIA:
THE BIBLE AND PUBLICATION SOCIETY,
530 ARCH STREET.

CONTENTS.

CHAPTER I.
The Subject Opened.. 5

CHAPTER II.
The Prize Won.. 17

CHAPTER III.
The Agency of Fire.. 31

CHAPTER IV.
The Gathering of the Waters.. 47

CHAPTER V.
The Rock-Building Period.. 60

CHAPTER VI.
Materials for the Black Diamond................................... 73

CHAPTER VII.
Composition of the Black Diamond................................ 85

CHAPTER VIII.
Adjusting the Essentials of Life..................................... 103

CHAPTER IX.
Poising the Life-Balances... 115

CHAPTER X.
Unlocking the Treasure 133

CHAPTER XI.
Off for the Mines 150

CHAPTER XII.
Around the Switchback 168

CHAPTER XIII.
At the Mines 183

CHAPTER XIV.
A Trip Under Ground 196

CHAPTER XV.
Mining the Black Diamond 211

CHAPTER XVI.
The Old Miner's Story 226

CHAPTER XVII.
Visit to a Shaft Mine 246

CHAPTER XVIII.
The Tragedy of Avondale 263

CHAPTER XIX.
Dangers of Mining 294

CHAPTER XX.
Home Again 309

BLACK DIAMONDS.

CHAPTER I.

THE SUBJECT OPENED.

THOSE who have read a work published some months ago, entitled "Home and Abroad; or, The Wonders of Familiar Objects," need no further introduction to the Dean family. But that all other readers may properly understand the principal characters with which they will hold intercourse in the following pages, their presence is again invoked that a formal introduction may here be given. Mr. Dean was the esteemed pastor of a large church in the State of New York located in a town known as Willow Brook. It was situated in a rural and highly picturesque district, the church being one of the oldest in that part of the State. The congregation was made up of an intelligent and prosperous class of citizens. They were mainly from a New England parentage, retaining much of the disposition, thrift, and stern religious virtues of their ancestors, a lineage of which they were justly proud.

Mr. Dean, while warmly adhering to the general statements of the creed cherished by his forefathers from a firm conviction of their scriptural soundness, had nevertheless mellowed down some of their rough aspects by a more careful study of nature under the increasing light of modern science. In their day astronomy, geology, and kindred sciences were but in their infancy, and had been seized by skeptics to lay sacrilegious hands on the holy volume of inspiration so dearly cherished by them as the charter of their rights and hopes of heaven. Prompt and earnest to contend for the faith once delivered to the saints, the pious fathers had rushed to the defence of the truth of revelation, unconscious that in some of their methods they were beating against the citadel of truth in nature, which is but another form of the divine manifestation. Receiving much of his training under the old régime, it was not surprising that he for a time rested in the shadow of its mistaken conclusions. But a further and more careful investigation of these subjects, with the new facts brought to light by Newton, Chalmers, Mitchel, and other eminent and devout scientists, had brought him, as it will other truth-seeking investigators, to the clear and happy conviction that all true science, whether involving mind or matter, but confirms and harmonizes with the principles of divine revelation. With this increased light, the study of science was a joy and an illumination. So clear to him was the fact that God is the same everywhere, in nature as in the word of inspiration, that he bowed with most devout reverence to the teachings of both, clearly making the distinction in purpose between the two records— nature revealing his wisdom and power, and the inspired word his grace and love in the greater work of redemption. With this sanctified conception, he was very diligent and careful in the study of both records, and equally as intent when the object of contemplation was the humblest tuft of moss or animated drop of ditch water as when sweeping the heavens, with a transfixed gaze, through some powerful instrument. He had ceased to tremble for the ark of the Lord, however roughly infidelity might try to jostle it by heaping up the objections of perverted science before its progress.

Of Mrs. Dean it could most truthfully be said, "The heart of her husband doth safely trust in her." She was a devoted Christian wife and mother, and very ardently beloved and honored by all who knew her—a power in the community, where her works praised her in unobtrusive acts of charity and kindness. She was an example to the old and a safe counselor to the young, blending the carefulness of Martha in her devotion to the wants of her household with the fervent piety of Mary in her worship.

Ella was the eldest of Mr. Dean's children, a somewhat sedate girl, but sensitive and sympathetic almost to a fault. She was an enthusiastic lover of the beautiful, and devotedly attached to music—a warm-hearted and consistent Christian woman, caring more to possess the adornments of the Spirit than to shine in personal decorations.

Minnie, the other daughter, was a few years younger than her sister, and was a perfect bundle of whims and oddities, sharp-witted, and with a great exuberance of spirits, yet full of generous and warm impulses. Often guilty of improprieties and under censure, yet she was the life and pet of the household. She acquired knowledge almost by intuition, but was always sure to arrive at the whimsical aspect of a subject first, though laughter and tears often struggled for mastery over her countenance.

Milton, the youngest child and only son, was now verging toward manhood. He was ardent and impulsive, and had been vacillating and discontented, cherishing the mistaken notion that home was a dull place, and must be forsaken before the real zest of life could be enjoyed. To cure this unfortunate disposition, Mr. Dean had brought into exercise all his skill and love of nature to educate the senses and mind of his son, and his daughters also, to behold the wonders of creative power which are scattered everywhere. In this earnest endeavor he had been remarkably successful. The process by which this happy conclusion was reached is described in the volume referred to at the commencement of this chapter. From being dissatisfied with home surroundings, and wholly wanting in a capacity to discover anything worth looking at near its location, Milton had become a very enthusiastic student, searching into its natural history, collecting specimens of its rocks, plants, birds, animals, and insects. He had in this way accumulated quite a respectable cabinet, and was not unskilled in the matters of science which his specimens involved. In pursuing the course which had proved so far successful, Mr. Dean availed himself of every opportunity to add still further to the gratification and improvement of his children, being fully persuaded that all time and money thus spent was more than repaid by the stores of wisdom treasured in their minds, and by the stronger binding of the home ties. The contents of this volume will set before the reader the manner in which Mr. Dean continued the pursuit of his object.

Regarding the religious culture of his children as

a paramount consideration, the father never lost sight of this purpose, whatever might be the subject of investigation. The fact that they all now cherished hope in Christ and were visible members of the church did not cause him to lose sight of this prime object, for he regarded the development of a higher Christian life in those who already believed in Christ as a special motive for parental anxiety and carefulness.

In pursuance of his purpose, it will be seen in the subsequent pages how steadily every investigation ends in an exhibition of the wisdom and goodness of God. However remotely the first link of the design might be hidden, or however intricate the gradual development, it was certainly traced up to the eternal mind and shown to exemplify the infinite beneficence. With this aim before the mind, a piece of coal to Mr. Dean was as pertinent a text as the sublimer wonders of astronomy. Indeed, few subjects could be chosen more susceptible of bringing out the riches and depths of eternal wisdom: in itself dark as the shroud that once covered the void of the "great deep;" but questioned as to its origin and purpose, a divine illumination takes place, as though once again the voice of the great Creator was heard saying, "Let there be light!" and, lo! the dark subject is glowing with celestial brightness. It is now seen what ages of preparation were devoted to building up a proper setting for the massive Black Diamond. A fused world blazed through countless years to form a nucleus, and then the mighty void of boundless, curbless waters rolled and dashed their maddened waves until they were gathered in the hollow of the divine hand and subdued to order and harmony by restraining barriers. Then all the vital energies of nature were put forth in one mighty miracle of growth, converting a club moss into a mammoth tree and a pigmy fern into a worthy compeer, and so multiplying their numbers that the very earth was hidden in the awful depths of vegetation. To complete the magnificent structure, over this is spread a new world, and the mighty gem is pressed into its sublime settings, there to wait through untold ages till the wants of man, for whose use it was prepared, should evoke it again to the light and bid it glow for his benefit, warming his hearth or melting the iron bands which had so long held it a captive in its rock-ribbed dungeon.

To appreciate the value and relations of a thing, it must not only be estimated by its own intrinsic excellence, but be examined in the light of the multiplied and marvelous agencies combined in its production. Thus considered, there is hardly an object in the whole round of nature possessed of more elements of astonishment than the black heap of carbon which we pile into our grates and furnaces. It is surprising that such an interesting subject has not long before this been put into a shape that would please and instruct both old and young. If it has been done, the fact has escaped the notice of the writer, or he would not have put this venture before his readers. Whether this work will reach the niche open to receive a proper monument to this humble but most useful servant of man, others must judge. He can sincerely declare this much—the attempt is an honest effort to make the best use of his materials. No boast will be made of the resources at hand nor the manner of using them, further than to state that, with a deep interest in the subject, much careful reading, and original observation, the author brings to the preparation of this volume an experience acquired in the issue of two previous works of a similar character, which have been received with a favor far beyond his most sanguine expectations. The same motives have guided his thoughts and pen over all the pages he has traced in this series of works—the honor and glory of God and the present and future well-being of the young. Higher motives he could not have; and if the aim has not been reached, there is a satisfaction in the consciousness that the attempt has been honestly and devoutly made.

To the author, the study of nature has been a passion and a delight, ever serving as a ladder on which an ascent heavenward was attempted. Devoutly standing at its base, and looking hopefully upward, the glory of the descending angel has often filled the wondering sight, and the quickened soul has sought to follow the bright companionship on its celestial return. If the reality has not quite reached the aspiration, there has at least been cherished a devout thankfulness that on so many occasions the quickened apprehension could truly say, "The Lord was in this place!" There has been a sweet realization that such sanctified communion with nature brings the soul very near to the gates of paradise. Feeling thus, the author gives this volume to the reader as his EBENEZER: "Hitherto hath the Lord helped me!"

As in his previous works, the writer has ever kept a twofold object in view—first, to communicate to all his readers valuable and pleasing information in some department of natural science which could be made available for the best purposes of life; and, secondly and mainly, to lead the mind to clearer and devouter conceptions of God and his wonderful works.

It is proper that due acknowledgment should be made to Lyell, Dana, Steele, Winchell, Miller, and others, for facts and suggestions. It should be stated, however, that the author does not wish to be understood as entering into geological controversies, nor as fully adopting the theories of some of these writers as to the precise length of time intended in the six days of creation. It is not absolutely essential to decide the question whether they must be considered six calendar days or vast periods of time in which the divine will was unfolded. In either case the facts are unchanged. It embodies the creative energy and wisdom of God, which is the lesson sought to be inculcated. God created the beginning and he will finish the ending, and it is a small matter to comprehend all that lies between these two points when God bounds them both and fills up all that intermediates. These views are held as established—the general agency of fire, water, and vegetation in fitting the earth stage by stage for the purposes of God. These convictions have been embodied in the earlier chapters of the volume, in Mr. Dean's conversations with his children previous to their journey to the coal-mines.

The question of the time given to each of the great preparatory epochs of creative development seems to be one of small moment. With eternity at his disposal, the Almighty is never under compulsion to hurry any of his works. A sudden completion of

creation might have illustrated more impressively
the omnipotence of God, but it never could have exalted
the wisdom of the Creator as does that all-pervading,
all-sweeping, unifying mind, gathering
up the grand results of one mighty age and linking
them to the fresh energies of a new epoch, making
all obedient to his sovereign will. As we mark how
God plotted out the earth in outline, and then filled
up the void by the slow accretion of ages, each serving
as the stepping-stone or foundation for something
higher, we realize as we never could by one mighty
act of Jehovah the "eternal power and Godhead"
of the infinite One. God may wrap a world in night
and shroud it with a boundless ocean, but in this
awful grandeur he is not so wonderfully present as
when his spirit moved upon the face of the waters,
and he said, "Let there be a firmament in the midst
of the waters, and let it divide the waters from the
waters." It was not the earth's magnitude, but the
subjection of its mighty possibilities to order, that
called forth the divine approbation: "And God
saw everything that he had made, and behold it
was very good." The devout mind will be awed
more by the beneficent unity of creation than by its
incomprehensible magnitude, while poor baffled skepticism
will utter its blasphemies because it cannot
fathom all the unsearchable ways of the Almighty

and search out and link together the great chain of causes, while striving to the utmost to sever every link that binds man to his Maker.

Let the reader decide which will be the most satisfying to the mind and conducive to happiness—to study nature only to be perplexed and baffled, saying, "When I sought to know this, it was too wonderful for me," or to see God everywhere and in everything.

> "There's nothing bright, above, below,
> From flowers that bloom to stars that glow,
> But in its light my soul can see
> Some features of the Deity.
>
> "The light, the dark, where'er I look,
> Shall be one pure and shining book,
> Where I may read, in words of flame,
> The glories of thy wondrous name."

While the aim of these pages will be to teach interesting facts in the formation of the earth, yet the main purpose is to set the Lord before the eyes, so that in looking at the revelations of nature we may behold in its whole circle of truths only so many ways in which our heavenly Father commends unto us his love: "For the invisible things of him from the creation of the world are clearly seen, being understood by the things that are made, even his eternal power and Godhead."

CHAPTER II.

THE PRIZE WON.

"HURRAH for Mauch Chunk and the 'Switchback!'" shouted Milton Dean as with a hop, skip, and a jump he rushed from his father's study into the sitting-room, where his mother and sisters were seated.

"Why, my son," said the mother, "how rude and boisterous you are! If you are not more civilized, you will be likely to get a 'switched back' without going so far to obtain it."

"Thank you, mother; I'm well acquainted with that route, and don't care to take any more journeys in that direction."

"Then manifest a little more quietness, and we shall listen to what you have to say with pleasure, for I judge you have something agreeable to communicate."

"I should think I have," replied the son. "You know, mother, I was bothered in choosing a subject for my composition for the prize examination, and asked father to help me. He told me to take the first thing I saw or thought of, and just then I was looking at the men putting coal into the cellar, and told him so. He said I could not select a better theme, and promised me a visit to Mauch Chunk and the coal-mines if I succeeded in obtaining the prize, and I've got it; and now hurrah for the mines, and won't I have a good time? In preparing my composition I had to read a good deal about the mines and miners, and I had no idea before that the subject was so interesting. I've often heard coal called 'Black Diamonds,' and thought it was ridiculous to compare such common black stuff with the precious gems; but I don't wonder at it now, for coal is really the most valuable."

"My son," said Mrs. Dean, "coal is not the only common thing in life which has been found on experience to possess more intrinsic value than many objects of greater outward brilliancy; and this will apply equally as well to character. Glitter and show have led to many sad mistakes in life."

"I think I understand you, mother," replied Milton. "We could dispense with gold and diamonds with less inconvenience than we could with coal and iron, and could better spare the poet than the ploughman."

"Yes, that is what I mean, my son. We could manage very well if we possessed neither gold nor precious stones, and, indeed, have proved this by experience, so far as the last are concerned, as we have never had any costly gems among our treasures. As to the poets, they are delightful companions along life's rough road; but if not another such rarely-gifted singer should ever be born, the world would manage to get along tolerably well. Exhaust our coal-mines, however, and the loss would be terrible. Without them, we could hardly build a single railroad or iron ship. The deprivation of luxuries is an inconvenience, but the loss of the real necessaries of life is a calamity."

"True, mother, and that was one of the points I made in my composition which the committee noticed in their report with commendation. But didn't I work on my piece! Why, mother, I wrote and rewrote it six or seven times. I first used all the big words I could get into it, and thought they sounded very fine; but when father read it over, he advised me to cross them all out, and then see how it would sound. Well, I did so, and really was surprised that it read so much better; and then I found out that a good composition is not made by a multitude of big words, but by choice thoughts plainly expressed."

"A very important thing to learn, my son. We say a thing in the happiest and most attractive way when we put it in those words which make it plainest to the understanding of the reader."

"Oh, mother, you ought to have heard some of the compositions. Such big words and such a jumble of ideas—it was really laughable. Dave Mills showed off his wisdom with the greatest assurance. He boasted of his effort, and said he was sure of getting the prize, for his subject was so profound and intellectual; and most of the boys thought he would. It was a big word sure enough. Let me see if I can remember it. *Idiosyncrasy*—yes, that's it; and then he went on with a grand flourish: '*Idiosyncrasy* is a peculiar status that characterizes the individual and constitutes his homogeneity, and prevents him from being lost in the great conglomeration of humanity.' He had a great lot more of just such stuff, and I couldn't tell what it all meant. I don't think the committee could either, for I saw them smile several times while Dave was reading. I tell you I was glad I had crossed out all the big words in my composition. . After Dave had finished his piece, Arabella Dobbs, who you know writes verses, walked out like a queen and gave an 'Ode on a Wounded Cricket.' Let me see if I can recollect any of the stanzas. I thought them more funny than pathetic. She began thus:

"'There was a cricket once that lived
Beneath a rotten stump,

>   Who broke his leg, and then he grieved
>   Because he couldn't jump.
>
> "'He sung his song both day and night,
>   A happy strain it bore;
>   But now he's in so sad a plight,
>   He'll never sing it more.
>
> "'So deep and bitter was his cup,
>   And humbled all his pride,
>   He chirpèd once, then gathered up
>   His crippled limbs, and died.'

Is that poetry, mother?"

"It is rhyme at least, my son, and that is about as much as can be said in favor of a great deal that passes for poetry."

"I don't think the committee thought much of Miss Dobbs' poetry, for I saw them smile several times."

"They pitied the poor cricket, I've no doubt," interrupted Minnie, "for it was truly unfortunate to have a broken leg, and then to be embalmed in such execrable doggerel."

"Almost as brilliant as some emanations from the brain of a little sister of mine," remarked Milton.

"Well," retorted the sister, "if they do emanate from my brains, I am glad that there is sense enough left to prevent me from exposing their shallowness by exhibiting my nonsense."

"But," continued Milton, "when my turn came to read my composition, I was so excited I hardly knew what I was about, and was not very confident of success; but I came out all right, and ain't I glad! Yes, three times—I have won the first place in the class, got a beautiful set of books, and, best of all, shall have a trip with father and a ride around the 'Switchback!'"

"I most heartily share in your gratification, my son," said Mrs. Dean—"more especially because of the evidence it gives of your improvement. I prize it more for this than for any value your reward may possess, however great that may be. And that reminds me, my son, that you have not informed us what your prize is."

"Why, mother, it is a beautiful set of Hugh Miller's works, just the books I've wanted ever since I read 'My Schools and Schoolmasters,' one of the volumes of the set."

"It is, indeed," responded the mother, "a very valuable addition to your library. In reading these volumes, you will learn what great success and distinction may attend the humblest boy who improves the poor opportunities which a life of the severest poverty and labor affords."

"I shall prize the books very highly, mother, and hope I may learn much from perusing them; but I was more pleased because the committee, in awarding the books, spoke so approvingly of my composition as not only well written, but also presenting interesting facts on a practical subject, instead of being in the popular style of fiction."

"A consideration of great moment, my child," said Mrs. Dean. "The taste for fiction has become morbid. Writers generally overlook the fact that nature abounds in themes which can be so presented as to possess an interest far surpassing the highly-wrought sentiment of the novel, as the set of books you have won will most strikingly illustrate."

"But now about the journey. When does your father propose to start? There will be some necessary preparations, which mother will have to attend to."

"Some time next week, I believe," replied Milton, "though the exact day has not been set."

"Oh, mamma," exclaimed Minnie, "I wonder if papa will let me and Ella go with him? I should so delight to see the mines, and to ride over the 'Switchback' will be grand. I'll go and fill his mouth so full of kisses that he can't say anything but 'Yes.' Come, Ella, and help me."

"I should be delighted to make the trip with father and brother," replied the sister, "but I don't think it will be kind to tease father into compliance."

"Oh, now, sister," said Minnie, "I know father calls me his little tease, but I'm sure he likes it, and really wants us to go with him, and is just waiting to have us ask him."

"I am not so sure about that, my daughters," said the mother; "it will cost quite an additional sum for four persons to make such a journey, and your father's purse is not often over-full. Besides, you have just been talking about new winter hats, which will be likely to take all the surplus it may now contain; so it is more than probable that you cannot be gratified in both of these indulgences."

"I hope Minnie will give up her wild notion," said Ella, "for I think it will be right cruel to ask father to incur any such needless expense."

"Needless!" exclaimed Minnie. "Which do you mean, sister—to cover the outside of the head, or to put something into the inside? You can make your own choice, but I had rather fix up my old velvet for the winter, and wear my waterproof for another year, than not to go with father. I had rather put my sense into my head than to make a sensation by what I wear on it."

"There may be sense enough in your choice, sister," replied Ella, "but I don't think there will be much sense in your conduct if you importune father into a compliance with your wishes."

"Perhaps," said Mrs. Dean, "if you are both prepared to make the sacrifice which Minnie suggests, your desires may be gratified."

"I'm sure," said Ella, "I shall forego any additions to my wardrobe as cheerfully as sister for the pleasure of the excursion with father, but I want him to do just as he thinks best without importunity."

"Well, sister," said Minnie, "you may do as you please, but I remember the story of the importunate widow in the Scriptures, and shall try to profit by her good example."

"And I will help you, Min," said the brother, "for it will be so nice to have you and Ella with us. Father was going to buy one of Old Tage's skiffs for me, and I will do without that to help along, and will tell him so."

"That is very generous, my son, for I know you have wanted the boat very much, and your sacrifice will aid materially in removing the difficulties in the way of your sisters accompanying you."

Minnie now repaired to the study, where she was always welcome, determined to try the moral suasion of kisses in securing permission to be one of the expected party. She crept softly into the room and up behind the father's chair as he was busy with his pen, and the first knowledge he had of her presence was a loving embrace and a pair of ruby lips pressed to his own.

"Well—well—my—pet!" he exclaimed, as he could get the words out at intervals between the kisses; "what is wanting now?"

"Why, papa, just what you are getting," was the affectionate reply of the daughter.

"Ah, now, you minx, you would not have father flatter himself that his old lips have so much relish that you shower your kisses upon them just for the enjoyment? No, no, I think there is a smack of wheedling in their taste, so out with it."

"Now, papa, I do love to kiss you just for itself, for you are a real dear, good papa!"

"Yes, yes, daughter, I will not question that statement; but just now there is some other motive that increases the number above the usual quantity. There is a little diplomacy in this lavish expenditure of sweetness, so you may as well state the conditions."

"Dear papa," said Minnie, coaxingly, "you are going to take Milton to Mauch Chunk and give him a ride around the Switchback railroad."

"Yes, my pet, I have cherished some such intention lately."

"Now, papa, don't you think it would be real nice to take me and Ella with you?"

"Oh, ho! that is what I suspected the kisses were coming to; and you, no doubt, flatter yourself that the pleasure of your company will be ample compensation for the additional expenses of the journey?"

"No, no, papa; we are going to do without new winter hats and fix up our old waterproofs, and Milton will give up his boat, so that will make up most of the money. Now, can't we go? Just say yes, and you are a dear, good papa!"

"Stop, stop, daughter! you will never make a good diplomatist. You are too abrupt and profuse in stating terms. Let us exercise a little more deliberation. I am not taking your brother to the mines simply for gratification, but for the purpose of giving him some valuable instruction. I wish him to learn something about the formation of coal, the manner in which it is laid away in the earth, and the process of getting it out for the uses of men. In doing this we shall have to go up and down steep planes, into dark and deep pits, and through long, dripping underground passages. We shall have soiled clothing and smutty faces and hands; and do you think this will be just the thing for two timid girls?"

"Papa, I cannot speak for Ella," replied the daughter, "but I'm sure I shall enjoy such rambles very much, and won't be at all in the way nor afraid. Besides, I shall learn a great many things that I have much desire to know. I have often thought, when looking at the burning coal in the grate, how wonderful that we should burn stones taken from the earth, and how strange it was that they should be put there. I have read something about it, and looked at the pictures of big trees that have been found turned into coal, and I should very much like to see them just as they are in the mines. Please, papa, let us go, and I'll bring back a whole heap of wisdom to pay you for the pleasure."

"Well, if I consent to your going, I suppose I shall bring my little blonde back as a 'coal-black rose.'"

"Yes, that may be, papa; but I'll smell just as sweet, and will try and be a thornless one, too, to pay you for your kindness."

"My dear child," said the father, at the same time affectionately caressing his daughter, "I have ever found you to possess more sweetness than thorns, so I suppose we shall have to take you along, and your sister too, if your mother can spare you both for a few days."

"Thank you, darling papa!" exclaimed the gratified child as, after a hearty kiss, she bounded away to tell of the success of her mission to her mother and sister, into whose presence she soon rushed, and clapping her hands, exclaimed,

"Oh, Ella, papa says we can go! Ain't you glad?"

"I shall be very happy to enjoy the proposed visit," said the more prudent sister, "but I fear you have teased father into a compliance with your wishes."

"No, no, sister, I didn't tease at all. He intended to take us all the while—I know he did—if mother can spare us both." This was said with an inquiring look at the mother, who at once relieved the anxiety of the girls by saying,

"Yes, my daughters, I shall most cheerfully forego your company and help for a few days, if it will afford you so much enjoyment, and instruction too, I hope. But if you expect to get off next week, our thoughts and fingers will have to be well employed to get you ready."

"As we are going to climb rocks and creep through dark passages," said Ella, "we shall want but little finery for our outfit, so I think it will not overtax our resources or our energies."

"Why," exclaimed Minnie, "does not half the pleasure of a journey consist in the fuss you make about it? We must go over the whole vocabulary of preparation—'worried to death,' 'at our wits' ends,' 'used up,' and 'never shall get through'—or the neighbors will think we are just common, humdrum people."

"That is the usual shallow way of fashionable society," said Mrs. Dean—"a custom which I hope my daughters will never imitate. There is always time enough to discharge properly the real duties of life, and all fretful and impatient worriments are not only useless, but wrong; and to make a pretence of cares that do not exist is a sinful reflection on Providence. . I think we shall have to manifest no such spirit in our stir of preparation, nor, I sincerely hope, in all the future cares of life. Pretence is only a thin covering, and never hides the shallowness of character which gives it a manifestation."

"That is just what I meant, mother," replied Minnie, "for I was not serious in what I said."

"I understand you, my daughter; for though you are a little whimsical and thoughtless, I trust you have been too well instructed to be guilty of such foolish pretensions. But now let us consult as to what preparation is needful."

CHAPTER III.

THE AGENCY OF FIRE.

"WELL, husband," said Mrs. Dean, when seated around the supper-table on the evening of the day in which the promised journey had been decided upon, "I understand you contemplate an expedition into the coal regions, which is to include all your encumbrances except—"

"There, there, wife!" interrupted the husband; "do not get up another argument for woman's rights based on the cruelty of husbands; there are no exceptions in the case if you will be persuaded to join our company."

"Now, husband," responded the wife, "why did you spoil so apt an addition to the stock of instances? Really, I shall have to put you among the cruel ones for thus thwarting my purpose to arraign you as one of the masculine delinquents. Why, just think of the enormity of your offence—compel a wife to decline an offered favor, when she was anticipating the pleasure of having an opportunity to say that it was denied her!"

"Ah, wife, if you were really serious in your statement, your conduct would be quite as justifiable as are many of the charges that form the staple of the strong-minded platform. But, seriously, I am really urgent for you to accompany us."

"Dear husband, I appreciate your kindness, but I shall very cheerfully be the home-keeper, as duty and interest both dictate; and I fear you have not acted wisely in deciding to take the girls with you."

"Now, mamma," said Minnie, "I think papa would have been acting real *cross-wisely* if he had denied us. Why, Ella and I have been planning all about it, and we are going to give up so many other things that we have almost made up all the expense, and that is acting *penny*-wisely, isn't it, papa?"

"I can judge better of that, my daughter, when I know the sum total of your savings. I presume it will be all right, however; for if your self-denials do not quite meet the expenses of the journey, papa will find out how many things can be dispensed with without discomfort which may save his pocket on some other occasion."

"No, no, papa," quickly responded Minnie; "it's just for this time. We are going to the mines now, and don't want some things which would be necessary if we were going to a party or a church."

"Ah, my pet, your political economy is too elastic and one-sided."

"Dear father," said Ella, "I shall most cheerfully forego many indulgences in the way of dress and amusements for the great privilege of going with you; but all our self-denials will not meet the necessary additional outlay of the trip, and so I beg you will not incur it, and I hope sister will not tease you any more about it."

"And what does my little political economist say?" inquired the father. "Notwithstanding all her deposits in the common fund, father may yet pay too dear for the whistle should he take her along."

Thus appealed to, the warm-hearted daughter was touched, and pressing her cheek, which was wet with tear drops, close to her father's, said,

"Papa, I don't want to go if it will give you any embarrassment and trouble, and I am sorry I've teased you about it."

Kissing the tears from the soft cheek of his child, Mr. Dean said,

"I love my dear children, and am touched by your affectionate regards and willingness to forego coveted enjoyments for my sake; but let us settle this matter. I have considered all the questions of time and expenses, and shall be more pleased to gratify your wishes than you will be with the indulgence.

And now the only questions to be considered are, can your mother spare you both for so long a time, and get you ready to go with us?"

"As to the first condition, husband," said the wife, "I can very cheerfully say, Yes; and as to the other, we will do our best to have all things in readiness. When do you propose starting?"

"In a week or ten days," replied the husband. "This will give you ample time for preparation, and enable me to enter into some preliminary investigations, which will prepare us more intelligently to understand the great facts that will come under our observation. We will look into some of the wonderful agencies which God has employed to heap up the vast mountains of coal over which and under which we shall travel. And to-night I propose to explain what agency fire has had in bringing about these stupendous results."

"Why, father," said Milton, "I thought that all fire had to do in the matter was to burn up the coal after it was dug out of the ground."

"Quite a mistake, my son; fire has served an important part in producing that which it now consumes. This we will try and search out, though the investigation will take us back to a very remote period."

After supper was ended, Mr. Dean and his family

repaired to the library, where access could be had to such authorities as he might wish to consult, and the subject for the evening was taken up.

"When any object in nature," said Mr. Dean, "can be tangibly brought within the scope of our observation, we have a sure starting-point for our investigation, be that object an ocean of water, a mountain of rocks, or a bubble of gas. Without this initial truth, all is theory and speculation, with results correspondingly inconclusive. In respect to the *genesis*, or beginning, of creation, both of these lines of argument are used. Speculation takes us into the illimitable regions of space to theorize about nuclei, nebulosity, condensation, and gaseous oceans, and there it keeps us still. The discussions have been long, noisy, and inconclusive; and if we are to take the spirit of the disputants as at all symbolizing the unknown conditions of matter at the beginning, void and darkness are still upon the face of the great deep. We shall probably never know anything of matter lying behind the sublime initial statement of the Bible: '*In the beginning God created the heavens and the earth.*' The mysterious fact hidden behind this divine announcement is the same as that which relates to the life of the body or the vitality of plants. We can deal with the matter which brings these incomprehensible facts to our knowledge; but how the one was brought into existence by God, or the other came vital from his nostrils, we shall in vain strive to search out. That both are sublime realities we know, and that they bring to us certain tangible facts is equally clear. All the wisdom of man can carry his researches no farther than the works of God shall lead him. Beyond is God, and who by searching can find him out? Reverence will unsandal its feet there, and worship. To go farther is presumption; and to question, blasphemy.

"Leaving speculation, then, to those who have a taste and disposition to continue the noisy discussion, let us begin where God has placed a finger-board for us. Looking at this, we shall find it so plainly inscribed that 'he who reads may run' in the paths of knowledge.

"Leaving the question, then, as to whether the primary nucleus of our planet was the fragment of a star thrown off into space or a nebulous condensation, we can start with the generally admitted fact, based on certain known indices, that our earth was at one time an incandescent globe,

'Mantled in flame, and blazing infinite terror!'"

"How do they find that out, father?" inquired Milton. "No one could be alive to see it."

"Do you remember, my son, when we visited the great iron-works near Philadelphia, that you picked up a fragment in the road a long distance from the furnace, and at once remarked that it had been in the fire somewhere?"

"Yes, father, I remember that very well, and it was easy enough to see that, for it was shining just like glass, and all full of bubbles, and stripes of different colors, showing that different substances had been melted together."

"In other words, my son, it bore unmistakable indications of igneous influences; and we should have known from this single evidence that a furnace was near, though wholly ignorant of its existence before. It is by just such testimony that we deduce the igneous origin of our earth. Passing down through the later series of the rocks forming the earth's crust, we come to the foundation formations, called primitive, plutonic, or metamorphic rocks, so called as expressive of the manner of their origin. These rocks are unstratified, devoid of any traces of animal or vegetable life, and have all the marks of fire as plainly stamped upon and interfused through them as did your piece of 'slag' which had been thrown out of the furnace. Having this fiery inscription as plainly written upon the rocks as were the blazing characters traced by the same divine hand which built them up on the walls of Nebuchadnezzar's palace, the geologist needs no inspired Daniel to give it an interpretation. This is the work of fire, he at once affirms, and begins to trace out the great purpose for which it was kindled.

"As a further confirmation of this fiery beginning, of the earth, we have the unimpeachable testimony of living volcanoes. These vast reservoirs of seething, melted rocks present to us, on a smaller scale, all the phenomena deducible from the relics of the great universal conflagration of which they are but the smouldering embers. They pour out their streams of burning lava, which cools, and we have new formations analogous to those on which the entire crust of the earth is resting. There is at first a bursting forth of a mighty subterranean caldron, and then a sweeping river, or deluge, inundates cities, villages, and surrounding country, drying up rivers and lakes, taking possession of their beds, or heaving up islands or mountains, and destroying all life that tarries within its terrible sweep. Then comes the cooling, the disintegrating, by frost, wind, and rain, producing an alluvial covering, and the life once destroyed again returns to redeck and beautify the desolation. In these well-known phenomena are epitomized the igneous agencies in the physical history of our globe, and the inferences are obvious."

"I should think," remarked Milton, "it would be a long time before vegetation would grow upon such a surface."

"That would be the natural supposition, my son, but facts prove its incorrectness. Nature has abundant resources to restore wasted or destroyed energies with surprising expedition. Within the knowledge of living men, volcanoes have poured their devastating floods of fiery scoriæ over lands which they have seen restored to all their former productiveness and beauty. Some years ago I visited Reading, in Pennsylvania, and remember walking over a huge plateau of smouldering refuse taken from one of its furnaces. It was composed of slag like that which you picked up near Philadelphia, made up of the lime used for a flux and the refuse of the ore smelted. It was drawn out daily on iron cars, and dumped over the edge while yet glowing with heat; there it cooled and became as hard and brittle as glass. The heat and gas were too oppressive to admit of long contemplation; and had I been asked what length of time it would take for vegetation to get a roothold on that seething vitreous accumulation, I should have responded at once by naming centuries. A recent visit to the same spot has proved how mistaken I would have been. Though it is but a few years since I was driven away from the spot by its fiery exhalations, on my return I stood in the same place to behold it quite overgrown with rank grass and herbage, especially abounding in gigantic specimens of the datura, or Jamestown weed.

"In further confirmation of the fiery agency in the earth's construction, we have the well-known fact of the rapidly increasing temperature of the earth as we penetrate toward its centre, exceeding one degree of Fahrenheit to every hundred feet. At this rate less than fifty miles would give a heat so intense that it would melt all the known elements of the earth's crust. If this ratio continues until we reach the centre, some four thousand miles, it is fearful beyond conception. This very deduction has led some very close observers to question the whole theory. But as far as we have demonstrated the fact, results justify the statement. Indeed, it is hardly possible to array a series of facts that would lead to a more certain conclusion. Every volcano, geyser, or thermal spring is a living witness to the fused condition of the earth's core. Some of these flaming witnesses, as Etna and Vesuvius, have been bearing their testimony for untold ages, and repeat it in burning torrents of lava every few years, that we may not become indifferent to their evidence.

"Of course in that fiery age of the earth's history, no form of life, animal or vegetable, could exist, and all moisture or water would be vaporized and dissipated. To make sure that this should be a lifeless epoch, the universal combustion sent off its oceans of carbonic acid gas, in which nothing that breathed could live, even if escaping from the seething ocean below. A world of fire beneath, an ocean of poison above, and darkness hanging over the dread loneliness. Yet though so proof against all intrusion of life, it contained the vast staple of all vegetable growth; but to make it available other forces must be brought into proper relations to it, especially water. But if a chance shower fell from the 'waters above,' it was sent hissing back to its elevated abode, as we see the water leap from the red-hot surface of an iron plate. The carbonic acid gas which the great conflagration had so ruthlessly expelled becomes, however, the firm ally of the defeated water; and these bitter foes of combustion return again and again to battle with the exulting flames. The poisonous acid was ever pressing down on the fiery surface, and the water, dropping its advance guard of showers, was gaining here and there a skirmish victory. After a period thus spent in feeling the foe, possession is gained of some stronghold, perchance a crater's mouth from which the sentinel flames had been for a moment withdrawn. Here a little lake is formed, and becomes the presage of a complete subjugation of the fiery agency, and the beginning of the watery epoch in preparing the Black Diamond.

"But as we have had a very warm subject and have become somewhat heated, it might be rather dangerous to plunge suddenly into a world of waters, and so we will defer the experiment until another evening."

At the close of Mr. Dean's recital, Ella said, with a shudder,

"The account you have given us, dear father, is a very thrilling one, and has made me quite nervous. The idea of living just above and so near such a molten sea is unpleasantly suggestive, especially as we do not know the exact thickness of the crust under our feet, nor in what moment or place the imprisoned flames may burst through."

"We have no special reasons for alarm, my daughter; but such dread disasters have occurred more than once in the world's history, as burned and buried cities fearfully testify, corroborated by vast islands of scoriæ heaved up in the midst of the sea. The partially exhumed cities of Pompeii and Herculaneum stand as dread evidences of such catastrophes. But these events occurred so remotely that we know but little of the details of their terrors, except as revealed in the exhumed palaces, temples, and baths of the doomed cities. These are certainly ghastly enough. Numerous skeletons, in all the strange positions which the impending ruin would lead them to assume, have been brought to light, moulded into the burning mass, with all the lineaments of their agony sharply preserved, some of them in such positions as proclaim the sinful indulgences in which they were overtaken. Their hands clutch the wine cup or the dice, or they are found with their feet on the sills of her door whose steps take hold on hell. No written history of a nation's social life is half so impressive as a day's wandering through these cities opened for the inspection and admonition of living generations.

"But these fiery exhibitions have had much later displays of their fearful energies. In 1783, there was witnessed one of the most awful of these events that has ever startled the world. In June of that year, Skaptar Jokul, a mountain in Iceland, covered with perpetual snows, burst open, and torrents of burning lava were poured out, swallowing up large portions of the island. Its broad stream, some six hundred feet deep, burst all barriers, and flowed with a resistless force all over the country. It took possession of the lakes and streams, filling up their beds, and buried towns and villages in one common ruin. In August following, a second eruption took place, completing the destruction which the first had so terribly begun. Of the fifty thousand inhabitants on the island, more than nine thousand lost their lives. The island has never recovered from the awful visitation. From that time until the present year the fiery agent has been giving frequent admonitions of restrained wrath, which but a few months ago again broke forth with fearful and destructive energy, and the island is now seething in the smoke and flames of the disaster. In 1815 occurred a still more disastrous phenomenon of this character in the island of Sumbawa, one of the Molucca group. It commenced on the fifth of April and continued in activity until the first of July. The explosion was heard for more than nine hundred miles, and the fall of ashes was so great as to crush houses forty miles distant. The floating cinders were so thick on the surface of the ocean that ships could pass through them with great difficulty; and out of twelve thousand inhabitants, only twenty-six survived. To add to these facts, which go to show that the imprisoned fiery monarch is yet intent on regaining his lost empire, I may mention that it was only last year that Vesuvius gave fearful evidence of its rebellious spirit by driving all the inhabitants from its trembling slopes, and covering up their habitations with burning scoriæ."

"Oh, papa," said Minnie, "is there any danger of volcanoes bursting out where we live?"

"I am not prepared to say, my daughter, that we are completely free from all danger of such contingencies, as there is unmistakable evidence that such dread events have transpired in our portion of North America; and in the regions of the Rocky Mountains living volcanoes are still found, though in a smouldering condition just now. But this much we have to quiet our apprehensions: it is generally conceded by those most able to judge and familiar with the facts that our region is least likely to be shocked by such a visitation of Providence."

"I was reading the other day," continued Minnie, "about the late eruption of Mount Vesuvius. It was terrible, and I shouldn't care to live in a country where a volcano existed, for fear it might some day take a notion to try its energies."

"I am rather inclined to the opinion," said Mrs. Dean, "that our sense of security from such a disaster will more than compensate for missing such a grand display of pyrotechnics now and then, so we will add that to the other advantages of our highly favored country."

"We beat all creation, anyhow," exclaimed Milton, "volcanoes or no volcanoes, and can burn up a city now and then, and then build it up again as big as ever, before the other nations get over their fright from an insignificant eruption."

"And with such a good opinion of ourselves," said Mr. Dean, "embodying, no doubt, the true sentiment of Young America, we had better adjourn our conversation, or 'all creation' may bring some apt instance to spoil our self-complacency."

CHAPTER IV.

THE GATHERING OF THE WATERS.

THE night following Mr. Dean's description of the fiery epoch was characterized by a thunderstorm of unusual severity, accompanied by a fall of rain that was fearful and long continued. The consequence was a very disastrous flood, which swelled the streams into fearful torrents, overflowing large portions of the country. The contrast between the early evening preceding and the breaking light of the following morning was very striking. On the one hand was nature in one of its most quiet and dreamy moods; on the other, a fearful warring of its angry elements. The difference between the two scenes was so great as to be almost beyond belief, yet it was wrought in the brief space of a few hours, and produced by the mere throbs of nature's energies. Need we wonder, then, at the results when all her powers are intensified and active through untold ages, working out the sovereign Will?

The morning after the storm revealed an epitome

of the deluge. The swollen streams had leaped their banks and were sweeping through the valleys with resistless power, carrying away fences, barns, outhouses, and, in some instances, even the small dwellings situated immediately on their banks. Mingled with the current, and struggling in the drift, were cattle, horses, sheep, and swine, while trees, barns, and other elevated places were crowded by flocks of half-drowned chickens and turkeys. The only contented-looking objects amid the general desolation were fleets of dissipated ducks and geese, making excursions into unknown regions, and stuffed to over-repletion on their plunder. Bridge after bridge shared in the general ruin, and came floating down in broken sections to add to the confusion and destruction of the scene.

Mr. Dean and Milton were among the first to give their aid to mitigate the disasters of the hour—a work from which they were not relieved until the approaching darkness of another night.

That evening, when seated around the centre-table, the mother and daughters plying their busy fingers with preparations for the contemplated excursion, Mr. Dean said,

"The exciting scenes which have to-day kept us so energetically employed will furnish us with an impressive text for our evening's conversation—the agency of water in modifying the conditions of our earth. We have had an exemplification of its resistless force when the exertion was but partial, not worthy to be compared with the majesty of the ocean as it now is curbed and bounded. But we must remember that the combined waters that wildly sweep over more than two-thirds of our globe reach not to the sublime power and dominion of the 'great deep,' boundless and unrestrained. To snatch the universal empire from its proud sceptre, Jehovah shut up the sea; he 'set bars and doors, and said, Hitherto shalt thou come, but no farther; and here shall thy proud waves be stayed.' What pigmies we were before the breaking forth of a few of its lesser springs to-day! It tossed away our strongest bars, and went on its way laughing at our impotency. As we stand upon the seashore when it

'Glasses itself in tempests,'

we get, perhaps, the sublimest conception of God's omnipotence, for it rolls its proud waves to the beach as though they would dash it from its foundation, only to be hurled back in wreaths of spray, thus spending its strength in vain.

"Now, it required just such a divine ministry to contend successfully with the empire of universal flames. We have often seen something like this in the history of nations: when God raises up some grand agency to accomplish a certain purpose, and invests it with almost omnipotent attributes, after its specific work is done, its very superhuman endowments make it unsafe as a permanent existence. When this is the case, God mercifully recalls the agent, or so restricts its powers as to make it a servant rather than a master. The purpose of the complete supremacy of fire was now accomplished, and it must be brought into due subjection, as its entire removal was not within the scope of the divine plan. He who kindled the flames could dash them out at once; but when he set them blazing, it was as means to an end, and that could best be subserved by a process of cooling and a gradual contraction of its dominions. Fitly chosen agencies are set to do the divine behest. The character of these has already been intimated, mainly produced by the very power which they were now called upon to subjugate. The direct result of all combustion is the evolution of carbonic acid gas; and this gas is in itself a most deadly foe to the combustion from which it springs. It is very evident that while the materials of combustion were steadily lessened by consumption there would be a corresponding increase of this gas, so hostile to combustion; thus the once dominant fires would be constantly decreasing. It would be vaporized and ascend with its burden of heat, only to be robbed of that burden in the higher regions of air, and come down again for a fresh reinforcement.

"There was also another agency at work. Whatever of moisture or water might have existed near the surface of the earth would be sent off in the form of steam or vapor. A temperature that could keep fused the rock-elements of the earth would, of course, permit no more volatile substances to remain in contact with it. But the vapor ascending into the higher regions of space, which is known to decrease in temperature with great rapidity the higher we go, would be condensed into rain and sent back by its own gravity toward the burning orb, only to be baffled in its attempts to find a lodgment on its surface while the intense heat remained. Thus for unchronicled ages this contest went on, yet all the while pregnant of the final victory to the persistent waters. The fiery antagonist was all the time growing weaker and weaker, while the two allied forces were gathering a corresponding increase of strength. By and by an acre of crust is formed, and a drop of dew or a spatter of rain is lodged there only for a moment and then exhaled again into its impalpable state. But the crust has been made a little cooler and thicker, and its borders extended. Another spatter of raindrops descends upon this vantage-ground, and a little pool of water is formed, and the fiery element, in its attempt to overlap it, pushes up slight edges, which the now entrenched waters fill up at once, and the pool is expanded into a lake, and the battle for a final triumph has really begun. How long this struggle between the opposite elements of fire and water continued, it is impossible to compute, as they have left no chronicle to guide us; but that it was long and fierce is evident from the discordances left in the plutonic rocks, which mark the grand scene of conflict. The cooling crust would be broken into craters by the imprisoned gases beneath, or into dissevered fragments by the tidal wave which followed the revolution of the earth, or by repeated contractions, only to be glued together again in larger and shapeless masses. In this period we can imagine the earth as possessing a globular form in its general outlines, but cramped here and there into slight inequalities, with little lakelets steaming with vapor, mantling around jagged peaks, broken and discordant, and changing continually. But victory after victory crowns the combined armies of carbonic acid gas and water, until the fire-fiend is bound hand and foot and placed in a prison of adamant, and the great deep takes possession of the conquered world, boundless and sublime in its undisputed empire.

"Mr. Steele thus graphically idealizes this epoch: 'Let us imagine the scenery of that primitive period. A dark atmosphere of steam, vapor, and sulphurous clouds, which conceals the face of the sun, and through which the light of the moon or stars never penetrates; an ocean of boiling water, heated at a thousand points from the central fire; low, half-molten islands, dim through the fog, and scarcely more fixed than the waves themselves that heave and tremble, lashed into fury by perpetual tempests; roaring geysers, that ever and anon throw up intermittent jets of boiling water and steam from the tremulous lands. In the dim horizon the red glare of fire shoots forth from yawning chasms, and fragments of molten rocks with clouds of ashes are borne aloft; incessant flashes of lightning, evoked by the vast chemical changes which are taking place, dart to and fro, shedding a lurid glare upon the seething ocean-caldron beneath; while bursts of echoing thunder, peal after peal, complete the grand but awful picture.'

"But," continued Mr. Dean, "it often happens that powerful personages, in the time of need, are glad to receive the aid of lesser potencies; but when success has crowned the combined efforts, the smaller allies in the victory are frequently treated with disregard or quite cast off. Thus the friendly carbonic acid gas, which had served so important a part in the grand overthrow of the fiery kingdom, was left without dominion and quite out of sight, to wait for a period when a more friendly alliance could be formed with an offspring of the now omnipotent flood.

"This event brings us to the era when divine revelation begins the calendar of organic creation. The first verse in Genesis only asserts the beginning of things, but does not imply that this event had just then transpired. Indeed, the second verse necessarily compels us to give it quite a different interpretation, and gives us full scope and sanction to deduce from known facts the general outlines of the two preceding epochs already described. From this onward, however, the Bible account correctly interpreted, and the facts of geology properly understood, grandly harmonize in their revelations."

"Oh, father," said Ella, "I don't wonder that God asked Job, 'Where wast thou when I laid the foundations of the earth? declare, if thou hast understanding. Who hath laid the measures thereof, if thou knowest? or who hath stretched the line upon it? Whereupon are the foundations fastened? or who hath laid the corner-stone thereof?'"

"Neither can any intelligent mind, my daughter; for one glimpse of the world is enough to make us stand in awe of God. If you will notice the verses following those you have quoted from Job, you will see how the statements of the Almighty correspond with the inferences made from the facts in nature. Mark the expressions: 'When I made the cloud the garment thereof, and thick darkness a swaddling-band for it, and brake up for it my decreed place, and set bars and doors.' God, who made all things, and who alone could reveal what was pre-Adamic, here intimates the vapory surroundings of the earth and the final gathering together of the waters upon its face into seas, curbed and restrained by the divine will."

"Yes, father," said Milton; "and I now better understand how the mind must be perplexed that does not recognize the hand of God in these things. I'm sure it is much better to say, 'God did it all,' than to sit perplexed, knowing not how or by whom anything was made. It seems to me the most absurd thing imaginable to assert that matter created itself. Isn't that about what the so-called development theory amounts to?"

"Most emphatically, my son. They may talk about development; but run the series as far back as you please, and it does not alter the fact—matter must in the beginning have had a creator or have created itself. There is no possibility of avoiding one or the other of these positions. Which hypothesis best comports with reason and common sense, putting revelation aside, is of easy decision."

"I should think it was," said Minnie; "and I don't wonder that those who deny the agency of God in creation, assert their descent from a monkey, for they ought to know their own parentage."

"Good for you, Min!" shouted Milton; "we'll send you as our missionary to the Darwinites, and perhaps you can develope them into a little common sense."

"Thank you, brother," was the sister's response, "but I must decline the commission, for I remember that the wise man says, 'Though thou shouldest bray a fool in a mortar among wheat with a pestle, yet will not his foolishness depart from him;' besides, I'm accustomed to keep rather higher company than monkey associations."

"You are not far from right in your conclusions, my daughter; to do otherwise would be casting pearls before swine. To argue with such theorists is almost useless, so we had better leave them in the hands of God, who may by the influence of the divine Spirit bring them to the light and knowledge of the truth. But let us see if we can trace out the purpose of the universal prevalence of water upon the face of the earth, for dominion was given to it to work out some grand design of infinite Benevolence.

"Of course no life could exist on the heated and bare surface of the first rocky formation, nor, had the surface been perfectly smooth, could any lodgment have been made by the very slight erosion which would have taken place by the action of the waves, to form a nucleus for a beginning of life. But the constant upheavals and the breaking up of the crust of the earth by gaseous pressure from below, and from a shrinkage above, would leave sharp points and edges and deep cavities, which the constant dash and roll of the waves would wear off and deposit in the hollows and eddies to form fitting spots for the first ocean gardens of seaweeds and beds for embryo mollusks. A similar process we see constantly going on in the wash and wear of our streams and all along our extended ocean shores and lakes; in most cases with much greater rapidity, for most of our surface rocks are much softer and more easily worn away than are the plutonic and metamorphic series. This marked difference in the erosion of rocks is seen wherever dykes of trap stand like vast towers or pinnacles almost proof against the tooth of time, while sandstones, limestones, and shales are swept away, forming soils for vegetation. The western shore of Lake Superior is grandly castellated by these intrusive dykes. All sedimentary rock in drying will crack and often leave large fissures, which the melted trap takes advantage of and fills up, creeping into every ramification, branching and curling, or shooting up into tall columns; and then the wear and tear of years removes the softer moulding, and leaves the adamantine casting as nature's statuary adorning the landscape. Fingal's Cave in Scotland and the Giant's Causeway in Ireland are world-renowned instances of this sculpturing of nature.

"Chemistry, no doubt, lent its efficient aid during this era of the world's growth. The fires beneath were still sending up immense volumes of carbonic acid gas, which went slowly bubbling up to the surface, being lighter than the water, but heavier than the atmosphere. This agent has a dissolving power on the rocks, especially those containing any lime, and would more or less aid the action of the water in the work of disintegration, and the laws of chemical affinity would help to reform the commingled sediment into gneiss, granite, trap, and other metamorphic rocks.

"We began our sketch," continued Mr. Dean, "with a world in universal flames, and have followed it through the great struggle until subdued by its inveterate foe. The mighty external conflagration has been quenched, and the fiery monarch imprisoned in the centre of the globe. We now leave the scene as a world of waters. One extreme has followed another, neither of which indicates the finished purpose of the Creator. The clouds are exhausted, the waters above are joined to those beneath, and what now? Was this change of agents made to destroy what the fire could not consume? In our next conversation we will try and trace out the grand purpose which has been so sublimely outlined. Thus far it seems but a wild struggle of incompatible elements for mastery, but God held the all-conquering flood in the hollow of his hand. It will work out his sovereign will, and then, in turn, be shut up and restrained, and made to become a fellow-helper. 'At thy rebuke they fled; at the voice of thy thunder they hastened away. Fire and hail, snow and vapor, stormy wind fulfilling his will.'"

CHAPTER V.

THE ROCK-BUILDING PERIOD.

WHEN again the evening lamp was glowing and the Deans gathered around it, Minnie said,

"Now, papa, please tell us more about the formation of the earth, for we have been ever so much pleased with your conversations. You have shown us the world burnt up and drowned, but somehow it has got out of both of these terrible troubles, or we shouldn't be here to listen to its wonderful history."

"Well, daughter, your inference is quite conclusive, and we shall have to see if we cannot find out how the great deliverance was brought about.

"It is very certain that fire had the first opportunity in shaping the materials for the earth's superstructure, and equally true that water has been mainly employed in building up its firm foundations. We can mark each period of its progress by the character of the materials used and the manner of their employment. If we examine some of the old baronial castles in Europe, we can tell the age in which the several additions were made by the style of the architecture, since each period has its particular type. With equal certainty we can fix the successive periods of the stratified rocks of the earth's crust. We can also find sure data for our conclusions at the base of any mountain or high elevation where fierce storms have raged and poured down their sweeping floods. Let us examine the results of such an event. First, the mountain torrent would tear away the black soil from the surface and bear it to the plains below, then the yellow clay or shale immediately beneath it, after this the underlying gravel, and so on, until a deep chasm was formed in the mountain and a corresponding filling up in the valley below with strata nearly identical, only reversed in order, the upper on the mountain being the lower one in the plain. This phenomenon is of frequent occurrence, and is not more uniform in its results and certain in its evidence than the lessons we trace on a grander scale in the rock-building epochs of the earth's history. When a careful person has examined two or three such phenomena, he does not need to go over the same process every time he meets with a notch in the mountain or a filling up in the valley. His previous examinations have given him the key of their formations. These lessons of nature are too uniform to be set aside by an occasional exception. When we find a sharp claw, we do not want the jaw bristling with fierce teeth to prove that it belonged to a carnivorous animal, nor when a blunt molar is brought to light need we continue our search before we are justified in affirming that a grazing animal has had an existence. From a single scale Professor Agassiz reconstructed an unknown fish, and facts afterward discovered proved that he was correct. In this way we trace the history of the rock-building periods with almost absolute certainty of conclusion. God has graven them 'with an iron pen and lead in the rock for ever.'

"Thus far nothing has been revealed by opening the rocky volume that need cause the believer in divine revelation to tremble for the authority of his sacred book. However astonishing the wonderful agencies may be that produced the earth in its present degree of perfection, they do not equal those combined in the sublimer completion and infinite perfection of the word of God, and this we should suppose, as the former but shows the wisdom and power of God, and incidentally his goodness, while in the latter is embodied all the fullness of his immaculate love. In one God organized matter; the other is his plan for redeeming immortal souls. But let us go on with our examination of rock-building.

"How long the 'great deep' existed in void and

darkness we have no means of knowing, not even approximately, but that the period was immense is evident from the work accomplished. But the time was not wasted, for down beneath the deepest fathom of the boundless ocean the waves were rasping off the rough edges and pinnacles which the imprisoned fires were constantly pushing up in their efforts to break from their confinement. The erosions must have been slow, yet what vast depths of débris were deposited before the first indications of life are met with, either animal or vegetable! The thickness of this *Azoic* or lifeless formation is unknown, but its vastness is shown in the fact that within its compass are built up the great seams of granite, gneiss, mica slate, primary limestone, talcose slate, hornblende slate, schists, and some other rocks. These mighty additions to the earth's crust are evidently the result of the action of fire, water, and chemical agencies. They are the first fine abrasions from the cooling ebullitions of the universal conflagration. Being so deep beneath the surface, and but little subjected to disturbing causes, they are deposited with great uniformity and evenness, and the laws of chemical affinity were permitted to have full scope in adjusting the matter into new forms. Could the eye of any one save the great Architect, who alone saw the end with no impatience to work it out, have looked through the deep darkness which hung over this period, it would have presented a dreariness that would have been appalling—no harmony, no light, no life! The groanings of imprisoned fires below, and the surging of curbless waters above! The detonating thunders of submerged volcanoes, and the crash of rending rocks! The scene is well depicted by the sublime opening of Genesis: 'And the earth was without form, and void; and darkness was upon the face of the deep.' But the 'Spirit of God moved upon the face of the waters,' and their utmost depths felt the divine influence, and order began its ministry below, and the mind of God took visible shaping. Near the close of this period of dread desolation the first form of life is called into existence. On the rocks the humble marine algæ begin to creep, and the protozoan to stretch its jelly-like arms. But how almost infinitely small and organless! 'And there was the hiding of his power.' The mystery of mysteries, however, has been revealed to the earth. Like its parent waters, it is almost liquid, but it lives. We may infer that it was at this juncture, when the life before only known in heaven had an earthly inheritance, that the 'morning stars sang together and the sons of God shouted for joy.' Let us look at this strange visitant to earth. The learned call it the *Eozöon Canadense*. If we are justified in forming an opinion from this first embryo inheritor of earthly existence, North America was the recipient of this mark of divine favor. This eozōon dwelt in a house of stone, being, in fact, little more than clots of jelly in stony cells, and significant only as the intimation of something yet to come, and, so far as now known, reserved for long ages in the future for its realization. The vast internal heat must have kept the ocean-wrapt surface of the earth boiling like a caldron, permitting few or no forms of life to exist, for even the poor lone eozōon is called in question when advancing its claims for the high honor belonging to the first born of living things on earth. If it really lived, more than thirty thousand feet of rocks were piled over its sepulchre before the next inheritor of its wondrous gift comes upon the stage of action, and that but little higher in the scale of organization—a simple mollusk. What a mighty expenditure of time and massing of rocks was this to bring in the first forms of insignificant life! A little shell not unlike a finger nail, called *Lingula antiqua*, the first ancestor of the *Trilobite*. This stretch of time, not to take into the account all the unchronicled ages preceding, if compared with the present known increase of the earth's thickness, is quite beyond conception. 'Ha!' the skeptic will say, 'the mountain bringing forth the mouse!' We can again reply, With eternity before him, God need not hurry; he can take millions of years to make a mollusk, and multiply each successive period of a new creation by the sum of the last, and yet has abundance of time for all his works, with a sanctified sabbath of divine rest between each grand epoch.

"As I have already remarked, it was near the close of this epoch that the ocean had its first show of seaweed, the prophet of the coming Black Diamond, born in the sea and bedded on the rocks.

"This grand period of rock-building was crowned with its layers of graywacke, conglomerate, transition limestone, and some other transition rocks. When the series was complete, there seems to have been a long period of comparative inactivity in the energies of nature, and then a new departure is inaugurated.

"It is interesting to state, Milton," continued Mr. Dean, "in view of the fact that you once thought there was nothing worth looking at around Willow Brook, that our neighborhood contains the first specimens marking the existing life of this period. You wished to visit foreign countries to find something interesting to look upon, while very distinguished and learned men have made long journeys from the Old World to see the marvelous things revealed in our own rocks."

"Yes, father," said Milton, "but I'm quite cured of that mistake, you know."

"I hope you are, my son; but it will not be amiss to point out these native wonders, as we have some of them in our cabinet.

"Here is a specimen of Black River coral, often found in immense masses and great perfection of form. These are the deserted palaces of a race of polyps, little jelly-worms, a slight advance on the organization of the protozoans. This long, horn-like fossil is the dilapidated home of the *Orthoceratite*, specimens of which have been found twenty and thirty feet in length.

"It is shaped like a long horn, with a number of thin partitions, but whether formed to accommodate the growth of one animal or a race of descendants is not so sure, though probably the latter. It is interesting to me as being the first geological wonder that arrested my attention in early boyhood, and led to my searching into that department of natural science. I have wandered for hours over the limestone ledges tracing out these long outlines, and counting the vacant chambers, and wondering what kind of a creature it was that once occupied them."

"Oh, father," said Milton, "I've noticed such things many times in our limestones, but had no idea that they once contained animals."

"They once were inhabited, without doubt, my son, as were many other similar forms of extinct life. The visitor at Niagara Falls will find its gray limestone rich with corals, crinoids, and shells, some of which are the most perfect and beautiful that the period furnishes, or that can be found in any part of the world."

"But, father," asked Ella, "I thought you said some time ago that these things were found only in the lower series of rocks. How is it, then, that they are now found spread all over the surface?"

"A very pertinent question, my daughter, which I will remember and answer at the proper time, when we see how God unlocked the casket containing the Black Diamond; but now let us get through the rock-building history.

"It is generally supposed that it was during the Silurian period that God said, 'Let the dry land appear,' the dawning of the third day of the Adamic creation. Mr. Steele gives a very graphic ideal sketch of this era, which you may read, Milton. Here is the passage."

"'Let us picture to ourselves the scenery of the Silurian Age. The air, damp with fogs and foul with noxious gases, hangs heavy over land and sea. The sun sheds a strange lurid glare. The land, faintly visible in the dim light, presents few attractions. The new-born continent is yet crude and unfinished. Vapor is rising in clouds from the heated surface. With no song of bird, nor hum of insect, nor garment of verdure, it is a broad, low, barren, rocky desert. Everywhere are seams and gulfs and ridges, rent and upheaved by earthquake shocks, and swept by volcanic floods. The sea is the only centre of life. The low rocky beach is garnished with innumerable seaweeds, whose long trailing branches rise and fall with the tide, while every wave strews the sand with shells and broken corals, heaped in lengthened rows like the grass before the mower's scythe. Trilobites, in swarming shoals, scull their tiny boats in animated pursuit of food. Huge orthoceratites lie quietly floating their many-chambered shells on the surface, or speed through the water with long arms spread to grasp their prey. The sea-bottom is gay with the lily-shaped crinoids that, blossoming with life, foreshadow the flowers which are yet to deck the barren earth. Coral reefs stretch away in lines of beauty where myriad workers toil to build their many-colored fragile homes. In shallow places, too, there is somewhat of grace, for the graptolites cover the muddy bottom with their quaint mossy branches, overshadowing mollusks that sluggishly luxuriate in endless profusion below. Yet as the long ages go by continued changes take place. The land rises and falls. The sea retires, and anon pours swelling in again. The scene of life shifts from one locality to another. The great drama of life and death has begun, and it is to be played while the earth endures.'"

"A very striking picture," said Mr. Dean, when Milton had finished reading, "and no doubt in some respects accurately depicted.

"After another pause seemingly, active operations are again commenced, and the earth receives an additional belting of rocks, which pushes it up into what is called the Devonian Age, or the period of the Old Red Sandstone with which Hugh Miller has made the world so familiar, and which forms the topic of one of the volumes which Milton has received as a prize. In thickness its average may be fixed at about eight thousand feet, and it is rich in fossiliferous remains, both as to numbers and perfection. The sandstones of the period may differ widely in color, but they are all easily identified by their peculiar fossils.

"At the beginning of this epoch, on the little points of dry land the fern makes its first appearance and the moss begins to creep among the rocks. The larger proportion of animal life is still aquatic, but much advanced in perfection of organization. The chief glory was a race of fishes, nearly all of the Ganoid species, scaly, with a kind of bony shield on the top of the head.

"As the age sweeps on, the waters continue to multiply their shelly and scaly inhabitants, but the great upper sea of carbonic acid gas holds undisturbed dominion above them. No air-breathing animal could exist for a minute inhaling its dread poison. But the little ferns and mosses that nestled on the few barren pinnacles of land drank in its plant-nourishing richness, and shot up into gigantic forests. Thin beds of peat were in time formed, and then thickened into vast depths of vegetable stores. Around their borders the peers of the California cedars began their towering growth, and the rocky superstructure is ready for the laying on of the first course of its carboniferous addition. What grandeur and sublime unity mark all the works of God!"

"Yes, husband," said Mrs. Dean; "and from your sketch I have realized as I never did before, how much more impressive the Creator's works appear from the vast time taken in their development."

"It is strange," the husband replied, "that any one should overlook this fact. No one great act of creation could give such a conception of God. When we contemplate divine wisdom superintending through untold ages antagonistic forces, controlling and harmonizing them as co-operative agencies in working out some vast design of infinite benevolence, then we are compelled to say, This is none other than God who doeth such wonders! And how assuring and consoling that the mighty God who thus reveals himself to man is our God! He will guide us even unto death, and afterward receive us to glory; 'Neither is there any rock like our God!'

> 'Rock of ages! cleft for me,
> Let me hide myself in thee!'"

CHAPTER VI.

MATERIALS FOR THE BLACK DIAMOND.

ON resuming his conversations with his family, Mr. Dean said,

"There is nothing more interesting in the study of nature than to notice the relations of one order of existence to another. Each one is seemingly distinct and independent in its own manner of development, yet on careful examination is always found to have a direct and beautiful relation to all other orders, creating thereby a mutual dependence so intimate that the withdrawal of one is a corresponding loss to all. Like the movements of a well-regulated watch, whose parts are all well balanced and active, Nature advances in all her domains; but interrupt the action of one department, and there will be a suspension or retardation of the whole until time repairs the damage. If we have no rains in May, the consequence is a short crop of grass; then we have lean cattle, high price of beef, and the calamity finally touches us when my children ask, 'Father, where is the beefsteak this morning?'

"Now, if there had been no great period of fire, there would have been no ocean of carbonic acid gas to feed a marvelous growth out of which the coal-measures were formed, pushing club mosses up into forest giants and dwarf ferns into towering shades. If this wonderful creation had not existed, there would have been no materials out of which to form the Black Diamond, and we should have to burn our pigmy forests to make up the loss, or sit shivering in the cold. So you see that when God kindled the great fire at the beginning he thought of us, and was fitting something to enable us to kindle a smaller one in our cooking-stoves or winter grates."

"Oh, father," said Milton, "that is a grand thought, and I thank you for it. Isn't that the way we should always try and search out what a thing is for?"

"Certainly, my son. In no other way can we have a just conception of the ways of God or be impressed with a proper sense of his goodness. To see no good design in a thing is to hold it in light esteem, and to disregard its producer. In this earnest searching after adaptations we often find out that what at first seemed a bane, and which even may be such in itself, is but the help to a larger blessing.

"I have before explained to you the mutual relations of the animal and vegetable kingdoms, especially that wonderful fact of mutual compensation and supply of the essentials of growth. The absolute requisite of one is carbonic acid gas, and of the other, oxygen; and most curious is the fact that each one produces in excess of its own wants the indispensable requisite of the other. Every breath that animal or man passes from the lungs gives a volume of carbonic acid gas to the air, and every exhalation from the leaf sends forth a quantity of oxygen into the atmosphere. A great excess of either element will be the destruction of the opposite kingdom of life, but a happy balance of these essentials will give the highest perfection of life and growth to both. In passing from a large excess of either of these gases, it is reasonable to suppose that there would be an abnormal growth of that form of life receiving its stimulus from the peculiar overbalance. If too much carbon is diffused into the atmosphere, there will be an overgrowth of vegetation; but if oxygen is unduly present, a gigantic and tameless generation of animals would possess the earth. This would be the easy induction of reasoning, and that induction finds its confirmation in the facts of nature which led to the formation of the coal-measures.

"We have already considered the agency of fire in advancing the earth to its intended purposes, and fire is the great producer of carbonic acid gas. What a fearful quantity must have been given off with all the matter of the earth in a blaze! Shut a man up in a close room with a brazier of charcoal or a scuttle of anthracite coal such as we burn, and either would produce gas enough in a few hours to destroy life. Such calamities, resulting from ignorance, are of frequent occurrence. Overcrowd a room with men, and shut off all communication with fresh air, and the same fatal results would soon follow. Now consider a burning world blazing through untold ages, giving off its incomprehensible volumes of the fatal gas, with no form of animal life to check its accumulation, and it is at once seen what a monster ocean of poison would be gathered, pressing down as near to the surface of the burning earth as the flames would permit. Of the terrors of this scene we shall have a faint example when we visit the mines, and learn what scores of unfortunate miners have perished by going into the pits where the dreadful gas has accumulated, though but a few hours had elapsed since they had been working there in safety."

"Oh, father," said Ella, "I shall be afraid, I know I shall, to go into any of those fearful holes. We might be killed down in those dark places just like the miners."

"It becomes us in all places," said the father, "to use all due caution, and it must require special carefulness when we enter the mines; but beyond that we need give ourselves no uneasiness, as we shall always be accompanied by some of the miners acquainted with the pit, who will not take us into any of the dangerous localities."

"Well," said Minnie, "I'm going wherever I can get a chance to go, and want to pry into every hole and corner of the mines; so you needn't leave me behind, father."

"No, I will not, my daughter, but think it likely you will have more occasion to fear the carbon than the gas, in which opinion you will doubtless all agree when you once see the miners coming out of the pits after a day's work. They will look very much as though they had just prepared themselves with burnt cork to begin the Ethiopian minstrel business."

"A little water properly applied," responded Minnie, "will soon bring us back to our white relationship again; and I would about as soon have that kind of painting on my cheeks as to daub them from a pink saucer or powder them over with rouge."

"Well, we may dismiss that subject," said Mr. Dean, "until the time comes to make the experiment, and go on with the history of our wonderful gem.

"As I have already intimated, the superabundant carbonic acid gas must be got rid of before the period of air-breathing animals could be ushered in. We have seen how this was gradually done in the watery element, which had been so far advanced that in the sandstone period fishes of a high order were flourishing. This was done by the minute conferva, balanced by the jelly-like protozoan; the seaweed and its corresponding mollusk and trilobite, and these in turn preparing the way for the mighty sea vegetation of the Silurian Age, when the *Phytopris* and *Anthophycus* stretched their hundreds of feet of stems and branches along the surface of the ocean, drinking up by their millions of hungry mouths their gassy food, and filling the deep with a foam of oxygen bubbles. It was then that God said, 'Let the waters bring forth abundantly the moving creature that hath life,' 'and it was so.' The balance of life in the great deep is nearly reached, and the divine Spirit that had moved upon the face of waters, evoking order and harmony, now rests upon the first appearance of dry land to perform a like miracle of beneficence. These divine energies had been working through most if not all of the epoch described in our last conversation, and the nucleus of terrestrial vegetation had been formed, at first, no doubt, small in size and bleak in appearance. But the mighty storehouse of vegetable food was so full that nature could afford to fatten all the members of the kingdom to their utmost capacity. Eat and grow were the two great conditions of that era, and well were they observed, as we shall learn before we get through with our investigations."

"Why, papa," said Minnie, "I think you are making real pigs of the trees and plants of that age. They had nothing at all to do but just to eat and eat."

"Yes, my child; and by so doing they fulfilled the purpose for which God had designed them. And seeing you have made so swinish a reference, we may use it to illustrate our subject. You are a great admirer of 'Harry,' our Chester pig, and love to feed him and scratch his sides with a corncob. Like the earliest growth of vegetation, he only eats and sleeps; but is that the only purpose which he subserves?"

"No, indeed, papa; for by and by he will give us some splendid hams and lard, and a couple of nice juicy spare-ribs."

"True, my daughter; and so the trees fed to give us a little pure air to breathe, and a cellar full of coal to keep us warm through the cold winter."

"Ah, Miss Min!" shouted Milton; "you're answered for once according to your folly. You were not quite so sharp as you thought you were that time."

"She was quite as sharp as her brother is becoming," said the mother; "so I think you both had better drop the subject, and let us listen to something more instructive."

"The new vegetable creation," continued Mr. Dean, "with which the Devonian period closed, was passed over to the carboniferous age for its full development—a process, like all the preceding epochs, requiring a stretch of time of which we have no other calendar than the marks of immense duration. Of this we may get a faint conception by a reference to a few known facts. By a careful examination of a single coal-seam six inches in thickness, it has been proved to contain more vegetable matter than the most luxuriant growth of the present day could furnish for more than a thousand years. And further, M. Boussingault, a French savan, has calculated that the vegetable production of our day takes from the atmosphere about half a ton of carbon per acre annually, or fifty tons in a century. Now, fifty tons of stone-coal spread over an acre of surface would make a layer of less than one-third of an inch in thickness. By this it is seen that a period of nearly ten thousand years would be required to form a coal-seam of three or four feet in thickness. Keep these facts in mind, and then remember that coal-seams are found of twenty and thirty feet in depth, with sometimes several series heaped one upon the other, with thick beds of slate and limestone between the measures, until the whole amounts to hundreds of feet. Nor is this always brought about by a vast wood-drift packing the vegetable growth of a large extent into a small space, for often the stumps of the trees are found in place just as they grew, and even whole trees, as *Sigillaria* and *Stigmaria*. The first of these trees are quite common in some mines, and often many feet high. Being sometimes found hollow, they have received the name of 'coal pipes' from the miners. These facts prove that all coal-beds are not the result of drift, but were formed by the vegetable growth being pressed down just where it grew. Now, if we multiply the series of slate found in a coal-field by the ratio just named, we can easily see what an immense lapse of time was devoted to its formation. Our sable gem was the result of no hasty freak of nature to get rid of its surplus carbon, but was carefully planned and built up by well-bestowed and long-continued periods of divine working. True, the deposits are not uniform, nor do they probably exist under all the earth's surface. The mighty

F

growth by which they were formed was no doubt confined to the great basins made by the upheavals of the earth's crust, into which were gathered the wash and drift of the ocean's wear. How it was rooted and fed, plucked and compressed, can be searched out with much certainty. Facts already known show that these coal deposits underlie vast portions of the earth's surface, extending under the bed of the sea and outcropping on the mountains. Our own country is thus enriched above all other portions of the globe, so far as is now known. From the Delaware to the Pacific, sweeping in a broad belt from New Jersey to the Gulf States, we rest on a foundation of Black Diamonds; and of some of the choicest specimens, as the anthracite, we are almost the sole possessors; and even with us this treasure is mostly confined to the regions of Pennsylvania which we expect to visit.

"From this glimpse," continued Mr. Dean, "we not only get an idea of the immense period of time involved in the production of the coal-measures, but also of the vast amount of vegetable matter used in building them up. This material had no visible existence in nature, and was withdrawn from the atmosphere and made palpable in its black mountains of treasure by the all-wise and benevolent Creator. No one questions but that God could have at once condensed the ocean of carbon into its present form of coal, but such was not the divine method; nor would such an act of God, as has already been explained, so strikingly exalt the attributes of the Almighty. In pursuing the methods of God's creative foresight, he had already provided the requisites, and had them in his storehouse ready for his purpose. A limitless sea of invisible gas was to be transformed into coal-beds of enormous thickness. Forests of gigantic dimensions, thick with massive palms and towering conifers, through whose deep shade streams should stretch away, with margins overhung with reeds and rushes of equally wondrous growth, were to be compressed into earth-ribs. No trumpet voice of the Almighty evokes the result desired, but a struggle is commenced between the gaseous ocean and infant vegetation, as it had once before been waged between a world of fire and a drop of water. What a disparity of forces—a germ of life and an ocean of poison! The beginning of both contests seemed to give little prospect of victory to the feeble but courageous contestants; but God was on their side, and with his aid the weak things of the world can confound the mighty, and even things that are not bring to naught the mightiest things that are. We should make a great mistake if we looked simply to the elements involved in the struggle, and formed our predictions of the result by a comparison of their inherent forces. God's resources comprehend all things, and each in turn may become omnipotent as God makes it the servant of his will. Thus endowed, a straw can beat down a mountain, a drop of water put out a world on fire, and a germ of plant-life drink up an ocean of poison. What is all this to him who 'stretches out the north over the empty place, and hangeth the earth upon nothing'? We may well say,

> 'How narrow is the utmost bound
>   Of reason's searching eye,
> When clouds and mist impending round
>   Shut out celestial sky!
>
> 'But Faith looks up, with raptured gaze,
>   Through all the gloom and night,
> To cloudless scenes beneath the blaze
>   Of God's eternal light.'"

CHAPTER VII.

COMPOSITION OF THE BLACK DIAMOND.

ANOTHER evening found the interested auditors of Mr. Dean waiting for their hour's entertainment. He began by saying,

"Could any one with only the comprehensive range of human reason have looked out on the scenes of nature at the close of the period which ushered in the carboniferous epoch, he would likely have exclaimed, 'To what purpose is all this waste of time and matter? Why these deep and dank bogs of peat, these vast savannahs of matted reeds and rushes, towering canes, mosses, ferns, and conifers? There are no animals to feed upon their succulence, nor birds to build nests in their branches. They are flowerless and fruitless. So far as reason can now understand, they are destined to grow and rot; and is this an end worthy of the sublime preparations for their production? Does this make evident the hand of God, and evince a unity and benevolence of design worthy of a Being of infinite wisdom? Indeed, there seems to be evidence rather that all this is but a magnificent sport of nature, a mere child's play, as when it sets up a row of bricks or builds a cob-house, only to see how quickly its work can be demolished.' To our narrow inspection this conclusion might seem to have justification, but to the Almighty a thousand years are but as one day; and the first movement toward present results we may need to seek millions of years ago in the dim past. When nature had given birth to a miraculous vegetable growth, the divine Hand dashed it out of existence by a grand upheaval of the earth's crust, and poured over it an avalanche of mud, gravel, and broken rock, and once more all was desolation, to finite vision, but with God it was the means to an end. Again moss, rush, fern, palm, and pine sprout and grow, and lakes are turned into peat-bogs, only to be overwhelmed by a like calamity, and the ages sweep on with no seeming advance in purpose or external beauty. But no time nor opportunity has been lost, nor energies squandered. The great Lapidary was all the while composing the Black Diamond, building it up layer by layer until its magnitude should show his power, as its substance would his goodness. No one marvelous growth of vegetation would exhaust the immeasurable ocean of noxious gas; and even if it did, if left to decay on the surface, it would restore the deadly element to the atmosphere. But see the wisdom of God! He locks up the captive element in its prison of shale and limestone, only to be released in safe proportions when man, under the pressure of his wants, should petition for its deliverance."

"Oh, father," said Milton, "how wonderfully God does work! The thought you have just given us is sublime. Only an almighty and infinite mind could act thus."

"True, my son; hence we can say, with the prophet Isaiah, 'This also cometh forth from the Lord of hosts, which is wonderful in counsel and excellent in working.'"

"Dear papa," remarked Minnie, "I've noticed that we can never be found in any condition but that the Bible has some text just to suit the circumstances. Isn't that strange?"

"Yes, in one sense it is, my daughter, but in another it is not. It is wonderful, received as an exhibition of the wisdom of God, but not strange when looked at as an act of God; it is just what we should expect from him. He could not do otherwise, for he produces the circumstances and gave us the word of revelation to instruct us how to meet the contingencies of life. The same God is revealed to us in nature as in revelation, and it is not possible that he should so manifest himself in one volume as to contradict himself in the other. But let us go on with our subject.

"Milton, you may get Hugh Miller's 'Old Red Sandstone,' and read what he says of the plants which form the bulk of the coal-measures. Here is the passage, and it is a good illustration of his descriptive powers. Dr. Buckland said he would give his right hand could he describe as well."

"'A low shore thickly covered with vegetation. High trees of wonderful form stand out far into the water. There seems no intervening beach. A thick hedge of reeds, tall as the masts of pinnaces, runs along the deeper bays, like water-flags at the edges of a lake. A river of vast volume comes rolling from the interior, darkening the water for leagues with its slime and mud, and bearing with it to the open sea reeds and fern, and cones of pine, and immense floats of leaves, and now and then some bulky tree undermined and uprooted by the current. We near the coast, and now enter the opening of the stream. A scarce-penetrable phalanx of reeds that attain the height and wellnigh the bulk of forest trees, is ranged on either hand. The bright and glossy stems seem rodded like Gothic columns, the pointed leaves stand out green at every joint, tier above tier, each tier resembling a coronal wreath or ancient crown with the rays turned outward, and we see atop what may be either large spikes or catkins.

"'What strange forms of vegetable life appear in the forests behind! Can that be a club moss that raises its slender height for more than fifty feet from the soil? or the tall, palm-like trees be actual ferns, and these spreading branches mere fronds? And then these gigantic reeds—are they not merely varieties of the common horse-tail of our bogs and morasses magnified some sixty or a hundred times? Have we arrived at some such country as the continent visited by Gulliver, in which he found thickets of weeds and grass tall as woods of twenty years' growth, and lost himself amid a forest of corn fifty feet in height?

"'The lesser vegetation of our own country, its reeds, mosses, and ferns, seems as if viewed through a microscope: the dwarfs have sprung up into giants, and yet there appears to be no proportional increase in size among what are unequivocally its trees. Yonder is a group of what seem to be pines—tall and bulky, it is true, but neither taller nor bulkier than the pines of Norway and America; and the club moss behind shoots up its green, hairy arms loaded with what seem catkins above their topmost cones.

"'But what monster of the vegetable world comes floating down the stream, now circling round in eddies, now dancing on the ripple, now shooting down the rapid? It resembles a gigantic star-fish or an immense coach-wheel divested of its rim.' (Since discovered to be the roots of the monster Sigillaria.) 'There is a green dome-like mass in the centre that corresponds with the nave of the wheel or the body of the star-fish; and the boughs shoot out horizontally from every side, like the spokes from the nave or rays from the central body. The diameter considerably exceeds forty feet; the branches, originally of a deep green, are assuming the golden tinge of decay; the cylindrical and hollow leaves stand out thick on every side, like prickles of the wild rose on the red, fleshy, lance-like shoots of a year's growth, that will be covered two seasons hence with flowers and fruit. That strangely formed organism presents no existing type among all the numerous families of the vegetable kingdom.

"'There is an amazing luxuriance of growth all around us. Scarce can the current make its way through the thickets of aquatic plants that rise thick from the muddy bottom; and though the sunshine falls bright on the upper boughs of the tangled forest beyond, not a ray penetrates the more than twilight gloom that broods over the marshy platform below.

"'The rank steam of decaying vegetation forms a

thick blue haze, that partially obscures the underwood. Deadly lakes of carbonic acid gas have accumulated in all the hollows. There is silence all around, uninterrupted save by the sudden splash of some reptile fish that has risen to the surface in pursuit of its prey, or when a sudden breeze stirs the hot air and shakes the fronds of the giant ferns or the catkins of the reeds.

"'The wide continent before us is a continent devoid of animal life, save that its pools and rivers abound in fish and mollusca, and that millions and tens of millions of infusoria tribes swarm in bogs and marshes. Here and there, too, an insect of strange form flutters among the leaves. It is more than probable that no creature furnished with lungs of the more perfect construction could have breathed the atmosphere of this early period, and have lived.'"

When Milton was done reading, Mr. Dean remarked,

"That is a very graphic description, and shows what cultivated powers can do. The writer, had he consented to squander his time like his early associates in toil, would never have enjoyed the pleasures of such a conception, nor have so delighted his readers in setting it forth.

"From his description, as well as from our own observation, we learn how favorable every condition was for the formation of the coal-measures. The earth seemed like one vast hot-house. The subdued but not extinguished fires of the centre of the earth furnished the bottom heat to stimulate into early and rapid growth, aiding the sun in its work. The carbonic acid gas was the great fertilizer, while the superabundant moisture completed the favorable conditions for an unusual vegetable growth. In some tropical jungles we may have something nearest akin to this marvelous development of nature, as in Ceylon, Madagascar, and in the South American hummocks, where ferns are now found many feet in height, and canes grow into tall fishing-rods, with bogs and peat-marshes of immense size and depth. To add to the productiveness of the carboniferous age, radiation was wellnigh suspended, giving the whole earth, almost, the benefit of at least a temperate climate. Dr. Tyndall discovered that the presence of a few hundredths of carbonic acid gas in the atmosphere, while offering little or no obstruction to the passage of the sun's rays, yet prevented almost entirely any radiation of heat; thus vegetation was stimulated by high and uniform heat from below and a corresponding temperature from above, combined with other conditions equally favorable to its marvelous perfection.

"The growth of the coal-measures was always

rooted in the clay immediately underlying the coal, converted into slate or shale by the process which transformed its vegetation into carbon. In this we can also trace the wisdom of God. The rank growth would of course exhaust the capabilities of the soil, and so God covers up the worn-out surface and renews it by a new deposit of fertile clay. Thus, as in so many of God's creative plans, a double service is rendered—the growth of the past is secured and a basis for a new crop provided. However rank the growth of vegetation might have been, if destroyed and left exposed on the surface, it would have decayed and been mainly resolved back into its original elements; and as more than one-third of vegetable productions is carbon, its gaseous poison would have been returned to the atmosphere, keeping it in a deadly condition for air-breathing animals. But deeply buried from light and air, and pressed under an enormous weight, it was slowly carbonized by internal heat and other chemical agencies, just as we now see wood carbonized in pits. If the process is properly carried on and the air wholly excluded, the coal comes out preserving perfectly the shape and texture of the wood of which it has been formed, with no show of ashes.

"During the burning the wood has simply lost its moisture and some other minute elements, but has retained its carbon. Thus God packed away the vast forests of the carboniferous age into our rich coal-measures, locking up the carbonic acid gas which they had taken from the atmosphere, and converting the poisonous bane into one of his richest blessings."

"But, father," asked Milton, "how can they tell that coal is formed out of vegetation? If it was made out of trees and plants, wouldn't they all be so crushed up that we could not distinguish them?"

"That is mainly the case, my son; the vegetation forming the coal-beds is compressed and broken, leaving only a branch here and a trunk there, with but rare instances of nearly perfect specimens. But it is an easy matter to reconstruct any of the varieties from these fragments, however widely scattered. We have a quantity of oak, pine, and cedar logs lying around our saw-mills which have been obtained from the hills and the cedar swamps. We noticed their characteristics of fibre, bark, and occasionally a piece of a limb. Now, when we go into the woods where they grew, and find stumps, branches, and tops of exactly corresponding structure, would it be at all difficult to reconstruct an ideal tree of all these varieties?"

"No, father," said Milton; "that would be easy enough, certainly."

"Not easier, my son, than for the geologist to take

the fragments found in the slates, limestones, and coal-measures, and to restore them to their natural forms, and reconstruct a carboniferous forest. In both instances the creation would be ideal and yet truthful. A little piece of rock brought from the bottom of a deep boring (Fig. 1) may have types

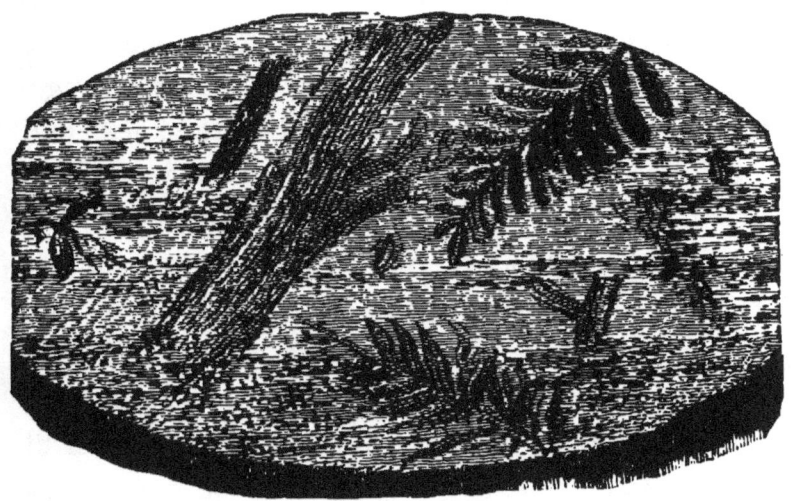

Fig. 1.—*Fossil Rock from a Deep Boring.*

of Nature's casting that will enable us to read the pages of her history yet hidden deep in the bowels of the earth. In this and other ways nearly all the materials used in constructing the Black Diamond have been brought before us almost as vividly as though we had stood among the wonders of their growth, and painted from actual scenes. Nature seems choice of her skill, and generally preserves patterns of all her handiworks, from the shell of an extinct diatom, only the one hundred and fifty thousandth part of an inch in size, to the towering carboniferous pines and huge saurians which followed so soon after.

"Perhaps our peat-meadows and the great swamps of cedar and larch which border on them will fittingly serve us for illustrating the formation of the coal-measures. In our peat-bogs the mass of vegetable deposit is three or four feet in thickness, and compact enough in most places to sustain our weight. But if compressed beneath thousands of feet of rocks and earth, there would likely be only a few inches of vegetable mould, but the forms of the mosses, ferns, and trees would be preserved intact. The unassisted eye might not detect them, but the microscope would bring them all out with wonderful distinctness. Here we have a lump of peat just as we now dig it from our bogs. Put this under an enormous pressure and then carbonize it, and though changed in bulk and color, all of its vegetable outlines would be preserved just as the charcoal preserves the form and grain of the wood from which it has been made.

"Let us search our bog a little farther. Growing in clumps, we find it studded with cedars, larch, and white birch, with borders overhung by giant sycamores, elms, and soft maples. Submerge these along with the peat, and subject them to the same carbonizing influences, and they would be incorporated with the mosses, pressed into their matrix, and blackened like it, but they would not lose their individual characteristics. The bark and fibre of the larch would be easily distinguished from the birch, and the elm from the cedar; and the compressed beds of rushes and alders would likewise tell the story of their origin."

"Oh yes, father," exclaimed Milton, "I see it all now; and isn't it wonderful how clearly these things can be found out? Why, it seems to take us back into those strange scenes."

"With a little help of the imagination, my son, we can get a very near view of those wonderful days. Taking the fragmentary facts which have been discovered, the whole landscape of the carboniferous age has been restored, and no doubt with great truthfulness. (See frontispiece.)

"Let us see how easy and truthful the process may be. The careful observer discovers in a bed of shale or coal a fragment of a branch of the lepidodendron, or club moss. (Fig. 2.) In another place the stump or part of the body of the tree is exhumed. At once he brings these fragments together in his mind, adjusts them according to what the facts of their growth shall plainly indicate as their natural relations, and very soon he will have the whole

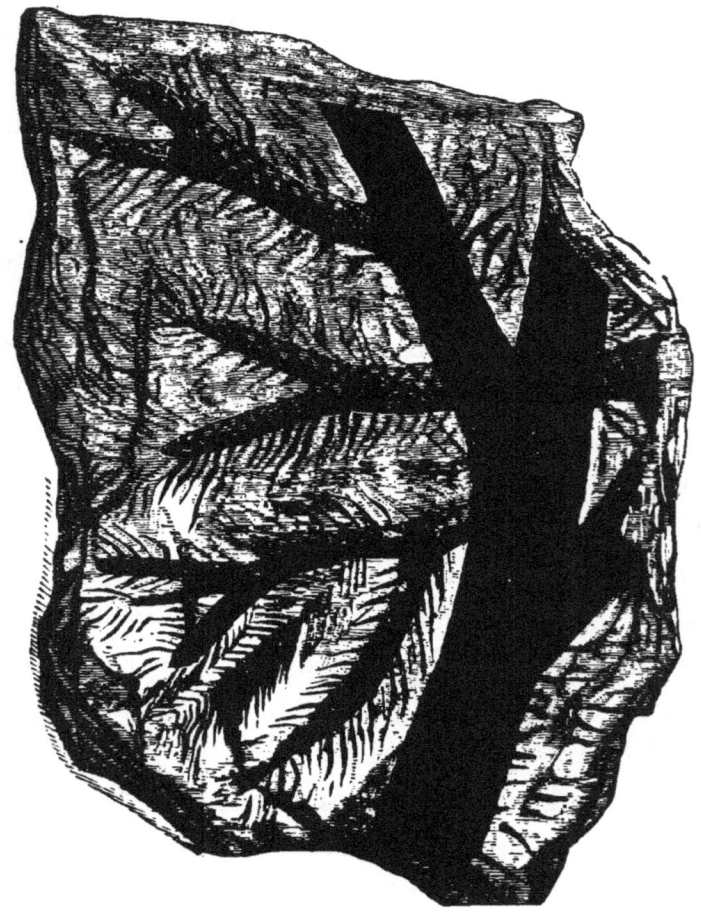

FIG. 2.—*Fragments of Lepidodendra.*

tree restored, in all its perfection of growth and form, needing only the color of its foliage and its

Black Diamonds. Lepidodendron.

pushing vitality to be as perfect as when it flourished in all its pristine vigor among its carboniferous peers.

"You can see a number of these wonders in the background of the ideal landscape.

"In another place is found a frond of tree fern, a calamite, a rush twenty-five or thirty feet high, a trunk of a pine, or a root or branch of sigillaria, and the work of restoration goes rapidly on until the coal-forest is growing before us almost as a living reality.

"It is one of the wonders of this coal-building forest that its trees were just of those species best adapted to the formation of the Black Diamond. Actual experiments have shown that while oaks, maples, beeches, and other hardwood trees will soon decay if buried beneath the ground, pines, cedars, and all endogenous or ingrowing varieties will remain unharmed for thousands of years. In the southern part of New Jersey a lucrative business is carried on by digging up the trunks of buried cedars and making them into shingles.

"These trees are found from ten to fifteen feet below the surface, and are very numerous near Dennisville and Tuckahoe. Many of them will measure four and five feet in diameter, being much larger than any of the living species now growing over the place of their sepulchre. I have examined an old dock in Florida built of palmetto logs, of whose construction the inhabitants have no knowledge. Yet it is still in good preservation and serviceable. Thus we see the divine wisdom in selecting the materials for our ebon jewel as well as in the marvelous manner of their disposal. The carboniferous trees were not only the least disposed to destructibility, but they also contained a larger proportion of the elements which could be appropriated to the formation of coal. Our hardwood trees use sap to take up the carbon necessary for their growth, which, being mostly water, is evaporated and returns to the atmosphere, and helps on the work of speedy decay, as is seen in the fact that what is called the sapwood always rots first; but the conifers and palms of the carboniferous formation were nourished by resins, which indurated and remained as the most enduring and combustible part of the mass.

"As we have already seen, the animal life incorporated in the coal series was plentiful, but entirely aqueous, and all the species except its fishes were of a very low order. Among its shales and limestones are many species of corals and mollusks. The star-fish appears, and the beautiful ammonite, varying from a minute shell to eight and ten feet in diameter. The fishes of the preceding epoch have advanced in number and perfection, and especially in size, the prophecies of the monsters of a coming age. But the most remarkable development of the period, which came near its close, was the order of reptiles. Like most of nature's beginnings, the earlier reptiles were small and harmless, but in their rapid progress, we find the most huge monster which the world has ever known, which will be the theme of our next study.

"Thus we have traced in brief outline the grand epochs which ended in the formation of our precious Black Diamond, and here it is in its various forms. We have lignite, the anthracite, the bituminous, and the cannel coal, each, as you see, with its peculiar characteristics.

"The work and the results are worthy of a God. He is omnipotent in all the operations we have traced out, and everywhere we stand wondering at the agencies and the ending, awed by the wisdom controlling the mighty works and melted by the goodness pervading them.

"Take up this piece of coal; in itself how perfectly insignificant!—a lump of black earth, useful to put into our grates, to cook our dinner, or warm our benumbed persons. In this light it has a small pecuniary value, and is an object of cupidity. But look at it again as the representative of God's power and goodness, invest it with all the wondrous stretch of time and the grand agencies combined in its production, and it becomes sublime in its suggestiveness. The dull lump of black earth is transfigured into a rich gem shining with a divine lustre. With this overwhelming conception we will close our present interview."

CHAPTER VIII.

ADJUSTING THE ESSENTIALS OF LIFE.

THE return of another evening found Milton and his sisters ready to listen to a continuation of the interesting recital which Mr. Dean was giving them of the formation of the coal-measures.

"We closed our lesson," he began, "at a very remarkable termination in the progress of creation, impressive from what had gone before, and quite as much so from what was to come. The often-repeated and marvelous growths of vegetation which marked the period just then closed had purified the atmosphere of its fearful excess of carbonic acid gas, and had locked up each subtraction securely in the depths of the carboniferous series, except the last and perhaps the largest withdrawal. To complete the work, a mighty avalanche, thousands of feet in thickness, of sandstone, limestone, conglomerate, and mud, is poured over the bogs of luxuriant peat, the groves of palms, ferns, and conifers, leaving a general vegetable desolation, and the period of the New Red Sandstone has begun, otherwise known as the Permian and Trias epochs. Amid the general submersion and desolation it is probable that a few points of land here and there were left, preserving a few plants or seeds of the vegetation of the previous age; but there was evidently preparation being made for the introduction of a more perfect and useful grade as the overbalance of the old should be slowly removed.

"It has already been shown that if the destroyed vegetation had been left on or near the surface, its substance would have been resolved into its gaseous conditions, returning all its poisons to the atmosphere. But this grand overspreading of rocky bars was too strong for all its power to sunder. In that deep prison-house it was doomed to remain until its life and poisonous breath should alike be destroyed, and a blackened skeleton alone tell of its existence.

"The conditions of a higher life, fitted for man and air-breathing animals, was an atmosphere of only one twenty-five hundredth of carbonic acid gas, combined with three equivalents of nitrogen gas and one of oxygen. The fiery origin of our earth had filled the air with a fearful excess of the first and most minute essential, while the grand process of purification by the marvelous vegetable growth which had been so securely locked up had given nearly or quite an equal excess of the last named gas; hence the perfect life balance was still wanting. Vegetation could eat up the poisonous gas, but in the very process it would give off a nearly equally fatal stimulant to life, and thus the vacuum was filled up by a new foe of animal life, and in some respects, perhaps, more to be dreaded. The malignant carbonic acid gas did its fatal work speedily; but oxygen, the new foe, betrayed its victims by promising a fuller possession of vitality, for its deluded subjects in the very moment of exultation found that the bands of life were not made strong enough to bear the tension of this excess. And now the question was, How is this new agent of destruction to be restrained and made to subserve, not to destroy?

"True, it courted life, and when it found aught that could burn or breathe gave the vital principle new and stronger pulsations. In bulk it was in larger proportion than any of the other elements in nature, comprising about one half of the material world. It makes up eight-ninths of the waters of the globe, one-fourth of the atmosphere, nearly one-third of all vegetation, and is largely present in all the animal kingdom. Oxygen has been called the 'matter king,' not only because it comprises the larger proportion of known substances, but because it tyrannizes over them all. It is a subtle foe. It comes unseen, tasteless, and odorless. Its guises are as numberless as the objects we meet, for it hides in them all, and it is only by sheer compulsion that it can be made to appear in its own proper character, and then you must keep it closely imprisoned, or, presto! it is gone with a flash. Iron, steel, and brass are no obstacles; if it can but get a spark of fire to kindle a flame, it will burn them as tow. Inhale but a breath of pure oxygen, and then breathe on the wick of an extinguished candle when not a spark of fire is left, and it blazes at once as brightly as ever. It has such an affinity for phosphorus, which is largely present in the substance of the brain, that if a piece is placed in the bottom of a jar of water and touched with a jet of pure oxygen, it will burst into a brilliant flame. From this we can see what influence an excess of the gas would have on all animals with large and active brains; and note the surpassing wisdom of God in the creation of a race of creatures, when it was so diffused in the atmosphere, with little brains but large lungs, thus using up the superabundance without danger of doing more harm than the agent which they were helping to subdue to proper restrictions. We know that all stimulation, within proper bounds, tends to growth and development. Thus we put phosphates and plaster upon our soils to stimulate the growth of our crops; and in like manner, good lungs and pure air—that is, where there is due proportion of oxygen—will promote animal life. If there is not enough of oxygen in the air, the poor subject is panting for breath, and soon dwindles and dies; but if there is a slight excess, there will be a corresponding advance in the increase of the vital growth. If the excess is too great, the fires of life burn too fast, and soon all its substance is consumed. Thus this gas would push the animal kingdom into a great excess of growth, as its fatal predecessor had the vegetation which it was to balance. In this gas we have a key to the first appearance of animal life in the water. This element has eight-ninths of oxygen in its composition to one of hydrogen; and though the primal ocean was undoubtedly much impregnated by the poisonous gas passing through it from the burning centre of the earth to the surface, yet it had enough of the life-essential oxygen to nourish its mollusks, trilobites, and embryo fishes; and as its submarine flora became more abundant to add its grand family of monster saurians, some of whom were to make the first venture into the atmospheric world above, where they have left their broad footprints in the primitive mud as they crawled along the new-born shores and made their venturesome experiments.

"Oxygen may be said to be omnipresent, and is essential to all life and existence, vegetable and animal, being an especial requisite of the latter. It holds the sceptre of the sea. And, by the bye, it is one of the most marvelous phenomena of nature, that water is mainly composed of two elements, one of which, hydrogen, is the most inflammable of substances, and the other, oxygen, the greatest supporter of combustion; and yet united—and we must remember that this union is not chemical, but mechanical—they become the greatest antagonists of fire. It is but another instance in which the divine wisdom is most miraculously seen in making the source of danger produce its own antidote. The destructive agent is made to work out the essential good.

"Oxygen is a little heavier than the atmosphere, and would of course take its place near the surface of the earth, which had been vacated by the absorbed carbonic acid gas. Through those long and vigorous growths of the carboniferous epoch, what incomprehensible volumes must have been given off! yet during all this time there was no demand for the excess of accumulation. No lungs panted for its vital nourishment. It was held in the hand of God for the time of need. He was tempering the breath which he was to breathe into the nostrils of a race created in his own image. We know something of the exhilarating properties of this gas by the antics which those manifest who have inhaled an undue quantity in the form of protoxide of nitrogen, or laughing-gas, which is composed of one part of oxygen combined with one of nitrogen, making the excess only one-fourth above the true vital balance; yet this would be sufficient to set the whole world crazy if the entire atmosphere were thus surcharged, which we have every reason to believe was the actual condition of things at the close of the carboniferous age. The exhilarating properties of oxygen have given it a medicinal value, and it is often used in some diluted form with good results in the case of weak and infirm persons with a low vitality, toning up their wasted energies, and is thought to be a good remedy for consumptives, enabling defective lungs to fulfill the required functions of healthy ones. We can appreciate its value after a lengthened run, when, amid our panting, we inhale a long breath and feel an instant relief, or when we pass from a close and crowded room surcharged by the carbonic acid gas from hundreds of lungs and drink in the pure atmosphere which God has provided. The beneficial effects of this gas, when regularly supplied in ample quantities, is seen in robust persons with large lungs. They grow large and fleshy, and often overflow with animal spirits. It is the safest and best stimulant which God has given. Yet even this can be used in such excess as soon to exhaust the strongest vital organization. If a multitude of men had been dropped into the sea of oxygen which followed the exhaustion of the excess of carbonic acid gas, there would have been a grand scene of lunacy, similar to what is often witnessed on a smaller scale at exhibitions where the laughing-gas is given for the purpose of affording amusement in the absurd antics which its subject displays. We had such an exhibition here last winter, and I remember you all enjoyed the occasion very much."

"I should think we did," exclaimed Minnie, "especially when Milton came out braying like a donkey; he did it so naturally." This was said with a meaning look at the brother, who at once retorted:

"Well, sis, if you had taken it, we should undoubtedly have heard the squawking of a young goose."

"Come, come, children," chided the mother, "I think you are both exhibiting something of the nature of the animals you name."

"Oh, we are only in fun, mother," replied Milton.

"We are guilty of folly enough, my son," said the mother, "without enacting more even in sport."

"Perhaps, mother," said Mr. Dean, "it would be better to let them go on a little while; they are only gassing away their excess of folly, and may settle down into proper sobriety when the fit is over, and then we can go on with our conversation.

"The whole history of creation which we have been tracing shows grand excesses subdued and neutralized into co-operating agencies of advancement. This is true of the superabundant element which held possession of the exterior world as we are now looking at it. All these adaptations have been slow in working out their ends. Oxygen is the prime condition of all air-breathing animals, but it must be tempered to their capacity and wants. They require an atmosphere where the general conditions will be a compound of only one-fourth part of this element, not an ocean of it almost undiluted. This balance must be wrought out somehow. If there are not multitudes drawing their vitality from the store, then there must be an extra capacity in the few which go to it for their supplies. How exactly this condition of things is observable in the successive introduction of the air-breathing races! The first living things began to filter the oxygen from the water, safe from the ocean of poisonous gas above. These lung-bearers grew larger, with more perfect and capacious organs, until the armored fishes made their appearance, then the batrachians, only a few inches in length, the heralds of the huge labyrinthodon, which should imprint his broad feet in mud many ages after. Then came the type of the mighty family of saurians, whose enormous eyes must have glared with a fearful stare at the frightened denizens of the deep, and whose wide and ter-

Fig. 3.—*The Ichthyosaurus.*

rible jaws were enough to make all lesser creatures flee away from them with the utmost speed. (Fig. 3.)

"We ought to be devoutly thankful that these monsters were confined to such remote ages of the world. They were grand oxygen consumers, and served their purpose; and then, fortunately for us, they slept with their fathers, and their sepulchres are with us until this day. Passing on through unchronicled ages, these and other amphibia increase in number and size, and drink up the volumes of oxygen as they come to the surface like the whale, their only living compeer, and the grand reservoir of vitality falls near to the true life level. We shall search in vain for any other conceivable purpose for these mighty and now extinct races. All other doors were effectually closed against the subtle element escaping from its vegetable prison, except such small portions as should return whence it came in a new growth. The water and the rocks had their due proportion of the vital fluid, and shut their doors against all of its importunity to make with them a habitation. But the atmosphere had neither the power nor the disposition to refuse entertainment to the new-comer.

"In the mean time the grand flora of the carboniferous age has been lessened in size and quantity. The overgrown mosses and ferns have given way to the graceful *cycads*, and amid their branches the first precursor of wings makes its appearance in an odd compound of beast, bird, and bat. The cycads in shape resembled the palm, but their leaves did not split lengthwise, while they unrolled like the fern; and being an intermediate link, it seemed to partake of some of the characteristics of palm, fern, and pine.

"This age has been most aptly called the Reptile period, and ideally restored with no doubt marked correctness, and on the same principle which has guided the geologist in reproducing the carboniferous forests. If we picture to ourselves the huge reptiles of that bygone age, it will make us thankful that we were not brought on to the stage of action with such surroundings; but we must not lose sight of the fact that this strange epoch in creation had a direct bearing on our future appearance where these scenes once existed; it was part of God's great plan in fitting the earth for man's dwelling-place by adjusting the essentials of life to his existence. And here we will close our chapter."

CHAPTER IX.

POISING THE LIFE BALANCES.

"TO-NIGHT," said Mr. Dean, on resuming the subject of the earth's progress, "we shall try and search out how God poised the life balances. Through all the long ages of an enormous vegetable growth, whose purpose we have tried to trace out, there had been an insignificant animal life struggling for a foothold in the earth, and recognition as a part of the divine handiwork, higher in organization and purpose than the mighty vegetation with which it contended. At first it was hidden away in the depths of the ocean, in almost shapeless masses or uncouth outlines. Now cleaving to the rocks as though struggling for its low sweet life, but gathering courage after ages of expectancy, it darts away with fin or flipper, exulting over its late vegetable neighbor, still fixed and motionless to its birth-rock. Still, the vegetable life sweeps triumphantly on; emerging from the floods, it fixes itself on the new-born hills, leaving its outstripped animal competitor, yet hidden and insignificant, to creep around its roots.

Surely this was not the life poise intended by the mighty Maker of a world that was to show forth his wisdom and power, and to praise him by an exhibition of its beneficent end.

"But ages roll on, and these wide extremes begin to shorten. Amid the vegetation, now greatly lessening in size, animal life has a corresponding increase in numbers and magnitude. It first timidly comes to the ocean's surface, and then grows bolder as the mighty saurians make the waves hoary and to boil in yeasty whirlpools after them. Still increasing in courage, it ventures to the muddy shores, and then climbs the hills exultingly, and sweeps over the vales, claiming joint dominion with vegetation. The scales which have been so long pressed down by triumphant plant-life are made to tremble on the beam. The balance is indeed near to a poise, but the animal weights seem to possess no value beyond their ponderosity, too powerful to be the prey of other forms of life below them, and nothing above them demanding a revenue from their immense vital stores. We can generally determine the purpose for which a thing is designed by examining its adaptations. Let us apply this rule to the huge monsters that once contended for terrestrial supremacy, and we will begin with the head of the list, the gigantic *Megatherium*. This monster was a huge sloth, living simply to eat and wallow in the cool shades of the luxuriant ferns in which he dwelt. (Fig. 4.)

FIG. 4.—*Megatherium Restored.*

"This 'monstrous beast,' as its name imports, must have been of proportions truly frightful. The first knowledge of its past existence was obtained from a bone found floating in the river Salado, South America. A hunter, seeing some large object floating down the stream, and supposing it to be the trunk of a tree, threw his lasso over it and drew it to the shore; but what was his surprise to find it a huge bone more than five feet through, being in fact the pelvis of some enormous beast then unknown. This, with other bones afterward discovered, served for the model on which the whole animal was restored and his habits found out. His fore feet were three feet long, while his tail was more than two feet in diameter. The creature must have been clumsy in form and slow in movement, but nevertheless a beast that one would prefer to meet as a fossil rather than alive in the forest. The *Megalosaur* (Fig. 5)

FIG. 5.—*Megalosaur.*

was a monster with legs nine feet in length, taller than a man on horseback, and from forty to fifty feet long, including the tail. This terrible creature was carnivorous, and could have gobbled up an ox at a mouthful; and what powerful jaws he must have had may be inferred from the massive muscles that surround the neck. Look at his head; there could scarcely be a quart of brains lodged within it, but what huge lungs must be in that great chest! and mark the wide nostrils through which he could draw in a perfect river of oxygen from the too largely impregnated atmosphere.

"But even this mountain of flesh was not equal to the *Iguanodon*. A restored skeleton of this frightful creature was exhibited in the crystal palace at Sydenham, and we may judge of its size by the following incident: by invitation, a party of twenty-one scientific men made a dining-room of the skeleton. The chief seat was in the head of the animal, in which sat Dr. Owens, the celebrated geologist, who presided. To build up the model and replace wanting bones, there were used six hundred and fifty bushel of stone, one hundred feet of hoop iron, six hundred bricks, twenty feet of inch bar iron, nine hundred plain tiles, and six hundred and fifty-two inch half-round drain tiles. For legs, four iron columns were used nine feet in length. The animal could not have been less than sixty feet long.

"In the Academy of Natural Sciences, in Philadelphia, there is the peer almost of this monstrosity, the skeleton of the *Hydrosaur*. (Fig. 6.)

"He was a species of gigantic kangaroo, thirty

feet long. He was evidently a land dweller, as his feet have no adaptation for swimming.

"But passing from the monsters which dwelt

FIG. 6.—*Skeleton of the Hydrosaur.*

mainly upon the land, we are met by an equally marvelous race of amphibia, living in the water and creeping along the muddy shores. Among these the

Labyrinthodon (Fig. 7), a monster frog, has left his bones and footprints to tell of his fearful dimensions. He attained the size of an ox, and from the possession of such a mouth, a perfect labyrinth of teeth, from which he takes his name, he must have been a terror to all his neighbors, whether on land or in the

FIG. 7.—*Labyrinthodon.*

sea. For a long time the footprints of these reptiles were taken for the tracks of some huge and unknown bird, but the true facts of the case have restored to this animal these marks of his past history.

"The *Dinotherium* was a curious compound of walrus and elephant, but with greatly multiplied dimensions. The lower jaw was more than four feet long, armed with an immense pair of tusks turned downward, and a double row of molars above capable of grinding up anything brought between them.

"Not pausing to notice many other huge creatures that vacillated between land and water, let us take a look at the odd companion of the *Ichthyosaurus*, already noticed, the *Plesiosaurus*. (Fig. 8.)

Fig. 8.—*Plesiosaurus*.

"This reptile was, as its name imports, a compound of lizard and seal, swan and quadruped, his tail corresponding more to the latter class of animals than any other. He was of immense length and proportions, but with a comparatively small head and little brain. What fearful conflicts must have taken place between two of these monsters or some of their equally gigantic companions! and woe to any smaller fry that came within their reach!

Fig. 9.—*Pterodactyle.*

"Entering the groves and looking among the branches or up to one of the rocky crags, what a strange object meets the sight! What is it, beast, bird, or dragon? It is the horrid *Pterodactyle* (Fig. 9), the original, perhaps, of the fabled flying dragon of the classics, and certainly quite as horrid in its terrible reality as the dream-pictures of the old poets. The creature was a winged reptile, with a spread of fourteen or fifteen feet, great claws armed with sharp nails, and a bill fearfully bristling with teeth. This creature was not unknown in our own country, for its finger bones have been found near Phœnixville, in Pennsylvania. Another creature, still more odd in form, but only of small dimensions, was also once a dweller on our shores, but whether more reptile than bird the learned have not yet decided. Let the question terminate as it may, we certainly ought to be grateful that we have more attractive objects in our groves. (Fig. 10.)

FIG. 10.—*Pamphorhynchus.*

He has a terrible long tail and a very long name, a shocking bad mouth, and a pair of wings such as were never seen before, nor do we wish them multiplied.

"But why continue this list of extinct monsters, when the question, no doubt, has many times suggested itself, What were these things made for, so gigantic in proportions of body and lungs, so small in brains, and so soon removed from the stage of action? We shall examine the question in vain, unless we regard them as designed to bring to an equilibrium the balance of life. The vegetation of the carboniferous age removed the overbalance of carbonic acid gas, but destroyed the healthy condition of the atmosphere by unlocking its stores of oxygen, that would raise up by its excess either a race of huge bodies with little brains to exhaust it, or a world of uncontrollable lunatics. We can see the wise and benevolent purpose of the Creator in ordering the former. The age of monster reptiles was but an oxgyen exhauster. Their huge lungs drank it in by floods drawn from the great ocean; and when their purpose was served, they were the race of all others which could be spared with least regret—nay, rather with thankfulness for their removal. If called upon now to give up some portion of the animal kingdom, we should most assuredly fix upon the remnants of these ancient reptiles, nor would we feel much regret in saying good-bye to snakes, toads, lizards, crocodiles, and all their loathsome associates. The dreadful ancestors of these tribes we certainly prefer as fossils rather than as living facts; yet let us acknowledge our obligations to them for the purified breath of life which they aided in handing down to us.

"It will be exceedingly interesting to notice the downward graduation of the ancient and gigantic reptiles as the balance of life nears its equilibrium. The iguanodon gives way to the mastodon and mammoth, and they in turn to the elephant, the mammoth leaving his frozen carcass in the icebergs of the North to inform us how recently he had finished his day of service. The megalosaur and the dinotherium yield their honors to the walrus and the sloth; the huge saurian to the lizard and the crocodile; the labyrinthodon is merged into the bull-frog; and the pterodactyle typified in the bat. In the mean time the mammoth vegetation has met with a corresponding decrease. The club moss once more creeps over rocks and old logs; the fern is but a foot or two high, the calamites is the horsetails of our ponds; while sigillaria, stigmaria, and many other gigantic plants have passed away, and are known only by their fossils. The work thus begun was carried on until the balance of life had brought the beam nearly to a poise, giving a regular and healthy life to both kingdoms. How distinctly we can trace through all this process the great fact that as the gross bulk was decreased the type was correspondingly exalted! We have smaller animals, but larger brains; a less growth of vegetation, but it is rich with flowers and fruitage. Does this indicate the contingencies of chance or the supervision of a divine, all-controlling mind? To the Christian the latter is a glorious fact; to the skeptic, the former an absurd delusion.

"We will not follow the upward series any farther than to say that the same divine wisdom is manifested in the means and results until the higher orders of mammals appear—that day in the progress of creation when God said, 'Let the earth bring forth the living creature after his kind, cattle and creeping thing, and beast of the earth after his kind, and it was so. And God made the beast of the earth after his kind, and cattle after their kind, and everything that creepeth upon the earth after his kind; and God saw that it was good.' And finally the perfection point was reached when '*God said, Let us make man after our own image, after our likeness.*'

"Since that day, whatever fluctuations may take place in the air, changes in vegetation, or ebb and flow in animal life, the atmosphere keeps its healthy equilibrium; each kingdom, as it takes away one element, restores another which it had for a time withdrawn, and on which the other feeds; so that chemistry finds the life-giving equivalents always present, whenever and wherever it may apply its searching tests.

"Mr. Steele, from whom we have already quoted, gives a stirring picture of the reptile age, which we have just been considering. You may read it, Milton."

"'It is the reign of reptiles. On every hand they swarm, crawling, hopping, stalking by the shore. The water is alive with them, swimming, diving, and filling the air with an indescribable din. All day long enormous lizards crawl through the forests, crushing the reed-like trees before them in their headlong course, or plunge into the sea, leaving behind a broad wake like a steamer, while others, more fearful still, spread their wings and riot in the air. Sailing in and out among shallow coves and bays of the coast, the plesiosaur, arching his long neck, eagerly watches a shoal of fish swimming near. But with quick, sharp strokes of its whale-like paddles, the huge ichthyosaurus darts into view, and glares upon its prey with its great bulging eyes. Instantly the swan-neck disappears under the water, and the plesiosaur is hidden from its rapacious foe— the terror of the mesozoic sea. Mighty dinotheria, rivaling the elephant in size, stalk along the shore or squat on the beach, stupidly gazing on the scene, save when the lælaps, with fearful bounds, leaps among their frightened herds, and tears them with his eagle-claws. But night draws on apace. In the dim recesses of the woods the pterodactyle—that winged dragon so terrible to behold—sails slowly along on its broad leathern wings. As the shadows deepen mighty sea-serpents dart to and fro, battling with the rising billows; that huge bloated frog—the labyrinthodon—jumps by with great ungainly hops, while a tiny mammal, the first of its kind, flies frightened to the shelter of the woods.'"

During all this interesting recital the family had listened with such unflagging interest that no interruption was made in the narrative, but now Milton said,

"Father, you have given us one of the most impressive lessons I have ever heard, and I thank you for it. I've often wondered what those huge and seemingly useless creatures were made for, and have never had any satisfactory explanation before. Your statements seem to me quite clear, though I don't remember having seen them anywhere in the books."

"I am glad, my son, that my discussion has pleased you and given you light on the subject. The ideas I have advanced are not new, but they have not been so prominently urged as I think their importance demands. By some they may be called in question, but to me they seem as plainly deducible from the facts as is the well-established removal of the carbonic acid gas by the carboniferous vegetation."

"I am quite certain, husband," said Mrs. Dean, who cherished the greatest horror of all the reptile brood, "that I am truly thankful that my lot was not cast when these dreadful monsters lived. It makes one shudder to even think that they once really did live on the earth. I could almost lose my relish for the air if I reflected long on the fact that it might have once passed through the nostrils of some of these horrid creatures before it came into mine."

"I do not suppose, my dear," said the husband, "that we get much atmosphere that has not served some other form of life before it comes to us; but it is preferable to take as little of it as possible second-handed. We ought to be grateful to the trees that so willingly distill the poison from the stale article, and give it back to us as fresh as when our Maker first breathed it into Adam's nostrils."

"Oh, father," said Minnie, with a shudder, "it almost makes the air taste fishy since I have been listening to you, and I wish I could banish all the loathsome cousins of the terrible creatures you have been talking about. I don't see what use there is for snakes, lizards, and alligators, anyhow."

"Perhaps not, my daughter, but he who made them had such a purpose in view that he pronounced them good; and though we may not be able fully to trace out the benevolence, their creation, I have no doubt, in some way subserves our happiness. Be this as it may, they certainly have their appointed place in the grand chorus of nature in adoring their Creator for the life which he has bestowed: 'Praise the Lord from the earth, ye dragons of all deeps, beasts and all cattle, creeping things, and flying fowl.' A voice that can adoringly join in the praises of God would be certainly missed from the choir, though to us the presence of the signer may be disagreeable and the part he sings inharmonious. If they accomplish nothing more, they at least enhance the sweetness of the harmony which their presence has prevented us for the time being from enjoying."

"I don't know how it is, father," said Minnie, "but somehow or other you always make a blessing out of every calamity."

"Well, my daughter, is not that better than to exaggerate the present affliction?

'Bowing to despondent mood
The sorrow only doubles;'

besides, we have Scripture warrant for such a consoling view. We are expressly told that our afflictions are designed to work out for us 'a far more exceeding and eternal weight of glory;' and that 'all things work together for good to them that love God.'"

"It must be true, I suppose," soliloquized Minnie; "but I can't see just where the snakes come in."

"Perhaps not, my daughter; but as God has given them a place with us, we must be content to let them remain."

CHAPTER X.

UNLOCKING THE TREASURE.

"TO-MORROW," said Mr. Dean, addressing his wife, as he took his seat at the supper-table, "if the Lord be willing, we will make our start for the mines, if you have the girls in readiness."

"We have but a few unimportant matters to attend to, husband," was the reply. "Comfort is exerting all her skill to fill your lunch-basket, which is, in her estimation, the most important thing yet to be prepared; and here she comes to report progress. Well, Comfort," continued Mrs. Dean, addressing the old colored cook, "how are the broiled chickens getting along? Have you got the basket almost full?"

"No, no, Mis' Liz'beth; dem two little chick biddies ain't mo'n tree or fo'r good mouf full, and so must hab plenty ham and beef tong' put in or deys go hungry, sure. But de bisket am jes so nice as yo nebber seed; dey's jes melt in dar mouf. And de krullers—I'se put de farwell taste in dem sartin. But jes see here, Mis' Liz'beth: dem gals am done gone clean crazy, to want to go down in dem dark holes. I'm sho we gets under de groun' quick 'nough widout runnin' way off to Mong Chong to creep down dar. I'se 'fraid Miss Minna 'll jes done get loss som' whar, she's so vent'som', and I can't spar' dat chil' no how, for I carries her right in my heart, I does."

"I think, Comfort," said Mrs. Dean, consolingly, "there will be no danger, as Mr. Dean will look after the girls and keep them out of the way of harm."

"Don' kno', Mis' Liz'beth; dem's right skeery places; dar's pow'ful bad spirits 'way down dar in de dark. Dat's dar groun', and it's right vent'som' to go dar. I looks mighty sharp, I tell you, when I goes into de cellar in de night, an' keeps out of de corners. But dem places whar Massa Dean am goin', dey tell me, am tree or fo'r hun'red foot 'way down in de darkness. I wouldn't go dar, sure. Massa Dean's mighty good man, an' de ole dragon don't cotch him no how, but he mout gib him a mighty big tussel, and skar de young ladies terrible."

Mr. Dean could not help smiling at the superstition of the good old cook, though he was deeply affected at her over-anxiety for his safety and that of her favorite child. As far as he could he relieved her fears by telling her that they would have plenty of light when they went into the mines, and would be accompanied by well-informed guides; so there would be no danger of their being lost or otherwise harmed; and as for the bad spirits, he had no fear of them, though they should likely see plenty of black folks down there, and be a little on that order when they came out themselves.

"Well, Massa Dean," the old cook replied, "I'se jes gib ye into de hans of de good Lord, an he's keep ye safe; an' my little lam' I puts right into his precious bosom, I does, and he'll gib her back to me. Yes, yes, honey, I knows he will," she said, in a subdued soliloquy, as she passed out of the room.

"Isn't she a darling old creature?" said Minnie as the door closed behind the cook; "and I do love her dearly if she is old, homely, and black. She has a beautiful soul, I'm sure."

"Love begets love, my daughter," said the father, "and that is a quality of the heart more beautiful than any outward adorning can ever be. But after supper I have one more lesson to give on the subject of coal before we see it in its native beds."

When the evening meal was over, and the cheerful lamp lighted, Mr. Dean said,

"You may remember that Ella, in the earlier conversations we have been having, asked how it was that the coal which Nature had buried so deeply was now found in many places on the surface of the ground, and sometimes even cropping out on the tops of hills. It was a very proper question, and I promised to answer it at a suitable time; this evening I propose to redeem my pledge.

"The coal-measures, as deposited, were placed near the centre of the rocky series of the earth's crust, and if left undisturbed would remain thousands of feet below the surface, and of course quite out of reach. Indeed, we should never have known of their existence; much less could we have made them available. But the beneficent One who had by such wonderful processes produced the treasure did not mean to lock it up securely from the sight and uses of men. He would do this only to fit it for use, and keep it there merely long enough for that purpose; then with the mightiest key ever formed he would unlock the precious store. It took a burning world to forge that key, and the hand of a universal earthquake turned it in the mighty rocky door of the treasure-house; and, lo! the black diamonds are set in the tops of the hills, crop out in cañon and ravine, and underlie the surface of the fertile valleys, rolled and bent, broken and piled, anthracite and bituminous, ready for all who might seek them in God's open storehouse.

"If left to do her work undisturbed, Nature is

the genius of order; she works by line and plummet.

"Had this been the condition in which the world was fashioned, the strata would have been uniform in thickness and parallel in their relations. This result is approximately seen in all rocks still found 'in place,' as the geologist designates it—that is, in unbroken, unheaved strata. But Nature has to endure rebuffs and opposition as well as mankind. She has a burning heart apt to burst out in fiery passions not easily cooled or quieted, and which has made sad rents in the bosom of mother earth. Earthquakes have given her a terrible shaking now and then, rending her rocky garments into sad tatters, and leaving more than three hundred unhealed issues over the surface of her bruised and broken body. In this way little has been left in all her rocky domains that has not been in some way more or less altered from its normal shapings.

"It is generally admitted that near or at the close of the carboniferous period a grand breaking up took place, which involved the entire North American continent, called the Appalachian upheaval. The bold marks of this stupendous event can be seen from Maine to Alabama in the successive mountain ranges, extending through the whole line, to which it gave birth. In some cases the coal-beds were sunken deeper than their natural position, but more generally they were pushed to the surface, or tilted up into mountain peaks, or bent into broad basins. In our visit to the mines we shall find the coal in every possible condition of form and place, showing how all-prevailing and powerful the great upheaval was which produced such results. The pressure of the pent-up fires below, and the weight of the great ocean above, exerted generally over the weakest parts of the earth's crust, combined with the lateral pressure east and west caused by shrinkage, were the great forces which built up the grand mountains of our country—the White, Green, Alleghanies, Cumberland, and other ranges in the East, and the grander summits of the Rocky Mountains of the West. These changes made miles of disturbances in depth in the earth's crust, bringing up to the surface rocks that were formed at the very bottom of the series and tilting them many feet above, sometimes lapping over on the later formations, which in turn became the base of the pile. Within our century events of a like character have taken place, though not on so grand a scale, yet they show the vast distances to which portions of the earth's crust may be lifted and depressed in a very brief period. In 1811 an island arose out of the sea off the coast of St. Michael's, one of the Azores, and was lifted up some three hundred feet above the surface of the ocean, bearing upon its brow shells and other débris of the sea; but in less than a year it quite disappeared, and now more than five hundred feet of water sweeps over the place where it once frowned upon the frightened mariner. Here was a disturbance of more than eight hundred feet, and must have greatly altered the geological character of the surroundings. As late as 1831, Graham's Island arose by volcanic action off the south-west coast of Sicily, and attained the height of two hundred feet, but this has also sunk back beneath the waves, and only a dangerous reef tells of its once grand existence. But in our own country, in 1811, an event of a similar character took place near the mouth of the Ohio River. The town of New Madrid, Missouri, was wholly destroyed by an earthquake, and the topography of the surrounding country entirely changed. The principal shock occurred in the night, and the boatmen employed in navigating the barges of that early day were awakened out of their sleep, and astonished beyond measure, to find their boats carried up stream by the broad Mississippi, which at sunset was pursuing its usual course to the Gulf of Mexico. I once held a long conversation with an old bargeman who was one of the frightened witnesses of this event. His boat was tied to the shore about three miles above New Madrid, and the hands had all retired to rest, save the single watchman, when suddenly they were awakened and startled by a succession of terrible explosions louder than thunder, and a fearful thumping of the barge against the shore. The water was boiling like a pot, and seemed to rattle like pouring shot on pasteboard. Soon a grand wave several feet high came rolling up stream, which dashed them from their moorings and bore them rapidly up the river, in which direction they were carried several miles before the wave had spent its force and the current of the river once more returned to its course. 'I tell ye, stranger,' said the old man, 'it made my har stand on end that time, and I began to think on my prayers!' The shocks were so violent that great chasms were opened in the vicinity, down which whole forests disappeared, lakes were dried up, and new ones formed. The channel of the Mississippi was changed, and now the river runs over the site of the destroyed town. The whole geological aspect of the country was changed. Fortunately for us, there has been no serious return of the fearful visitation.

"Numerous instances of great depressions of country have occurred as well as grand upheavals, and they accomplish the same results in unlocking the hidden treasures of the earth. Not to mention others, in 1819 a region of two thousand square miles near the mouth of the Indus was submerged, and the Ullah Bund, a noted mound, was upheaved near by.

"Abundance of facts like these show that the earth has passed through many grand convulsions, disrupting its rocky surroundings, and in some instances extinguishing its entire animal life. Thus the earliest mollusks and trilobites were dashed out of existence by some sudden and overwhelming catastrophe, and the latter are now found in vast sepulchral heaps, with the distorted lines of their sudden death as plainly and sharply defined as is seen in the human models found in the indurated lava of Pompeii or Herculaneum. It is also supposed by some geologists that the huge creatures we were recently talking about were swept from the earth by some such overwhelming convulsion. But let us pass on.

"Rocks are said to be 'in place' when they remain just as they were deposited, and, if stratified, preserve their laminæ unbroken. Where this form of rocks exists to any great extent we know there have been but few and partial disturbances. Of course we can never find the coal-measures in this condition, except where half of a 'fault' has been pushed up or a bed tilted to the surface. Sometimes the bed is bent into oval or overlaps itself, as is beautifully seen in the coal-beds of Locustdale, which we may visit before we return. (Fig. 11.) The dotted line at the top of this drawing will show the strata cut away by erosion; the experienced miner, knowing this, cuts a gangway across from one stratum to the other, as shown by the two straight lines. But perhaps the most common form in which the coal-beds are found

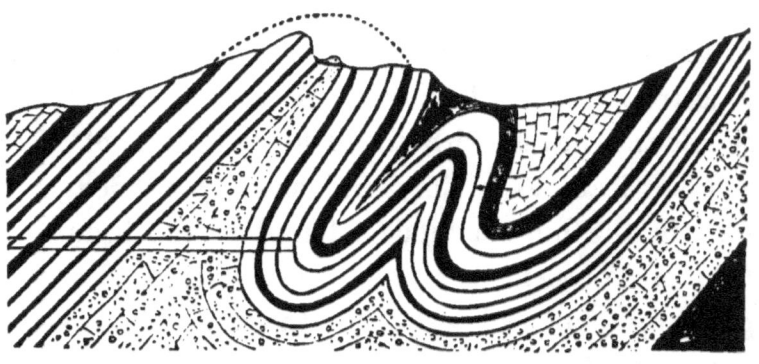

FIG. 11.—*Overlapped Strata.*

is in grand basins, the bottoms of which consist of the series 'in place,' with the sides bent up until they come to the surface. In this case the coal is mined by following the dip as far down as it is safe or profitable. When we visit the coal-fields, we shall find many instances illustrating the various formations, which I will point out to you when on the ground, and, as we may often be, when under it also; so we will pass the subject for the present.

"Not only are the treasures of coal brought within practical reach by this almost universal upheaval, but also many of the ores, the granites, and other very valuable rocks. Besides, we are indebted to this at first seeming calamity for most of the grand scenery of the world. Without this vast breaking up of the deep foundations, and tilting up of the various strata, the earth would have been a seeming dead level, painfully monotonous, as now witnessed in some of the vast prairies of the West—no Alps nor Andes, Alleghanies nor Rocky Mountains; no deep cañons nor mighty cataracts; no vale of Chamouni nor Yosemite Valley. We owe a great debt to the fire beneath and the waters above for their æsthetic labors. What one has pushed up rough and jagged the other has rounded off and moulded into forms of grandeur and beauty, and together they have sculptured mountain statuary and mapped out landscapes that are as much a part of the world's treasures as the more material wealth once hidden in the depths below, which they have exposed. The regions which we shall visit, in their grandeur of outlines and surpassing beauty, will impress us most profoundly with this truth. Mauch Chunk has been called the 'Switzerland of America,' and not without possessing high claims to the honor. Its scenes are not as magnificent and sublime as the Rocky Mountains and the Yosemite, but they are worthy of a comparison with these far western wonders. But we must remember that even these were fashioned by the same agencies. What a mighty hand must have upheaved the grand summits of the Mah-ta or Cap of Liberty! This sublime peak is four thousand six hundred feet high, and what an enchanting landscape it makes, with its bridal-veil-like falls in the foreground! Standing on its summit, or looking up from its water-worn base to its cloud-covered top, who but would forget all about coal, silver-mines, or even gold-dust, and devoutly thank God for the grand picture which the Almighty has traced out for the eyes to feast upon? Pass from this mighty sculpture of Nature, and look down the deep chasm of the Eagle Rock, of one thousand one hundred feet in depth; yet so near together are the giant walls that large boulders are caught and held midway. Look through the chasm to the wider opening beyond, and who can help feeling that the hand of the Almighty had been laid upon its brow and by one grasp of Omnipotence its firm adamant rent to its foundations? 'Surely the mountain falling cometh to naught, and the rock is removed out of his place!'

"Niagara Falls is but another grand instance resulting from the upheavals and erosions of the rocks; so is Watkins' Glen and the beautiful island of

Mackinac, on which are situated two of the most picturesque formations resulting from these wonderful agencies. On the principal plateau of the island a rocky pinnacle rises, like a church-spire, to the altitude of one hundred and thirty-four feet. It is a mass of brecciated limestone; and being harder than the rocks surrounding it, the waters of the lake that once flowed around it, and whose marks are plainly visible, have eroded them, and left this tall monument standing for wondering thousands to gaze upon. It has many crevices in its almost perpendicular sides in which years ago a few struggling dwarf cedars were growing. When but a lad, in company with several others, I visited this great curiosity, and we had all to show our skill and bravery by trying to climb to its top. It was a tedious and dangerous operation, and nearly proved fatal in my case. Determined not to be outdone by others, I succeeded in keeping ahead of them, and climbed so near the top as to be able to put my hand upon it. To go farther was impossible, and I soon found to my horror that it seemed equally so to return. My companions all reached the ground in safety, but there I clung to a small projection near the top, incapable of getting the least foothold below, and all the while becoming weaker and weaker by my fruitless struggles. It was in the days when vessels rarely visited the island, and the time soon painfully passed until the hour was near when the boat on which we were passengers would leave for Detroit. Down I must get somehow, or I should soon be left to struggle alone. Requesting my frightened companions below to spread a large and thick heap of cedar and spruce boughs at the base of the rock, so that if I fell I might be saved from being dashed on the broken rocks, then taking hold of the top of a small cedar that grew in the crevice on which I stood, in sheer desperation I let go my foothold and dropped down as far as the bush would allow, uncertain whether it would sustain my weight, and if it did, whether I could find another cleft for my feet. Fortunately, both contingencies proved favorable, or I probably should not have been here to relate the incident. The experience, however, thoroughly cured me of any further ambition for climbing rocks just for the glory of the thing."

"I trust the incident," said Mrs. Dean, "may teach our son a lesson of prudence. It was but a few days ago I heard him boasting of some wonderful feat in climbing the 'Eagle's Cliff,' for which his only reward was tired limbs and torn clothes."

"But, mother," responded the son, "there wasn't much danger in that operation, and it was some glory to leave my name above all the rest."

"A glory, my son," said Mr. Dean, "that I am sorry so many of my countrymen have a vain desire to reach, as is shown whether we climb the Alps or the Pyramids, or wander through the temples of Egypt or the old castles of Europe. Away up somewhere, in chalk or charcoal characters, you are sure to find John Smith or Peter Jenkins inscribed, with the inevitable affix of Slabtown or Mugginsville, U. S. A. If they would only leave off these honored initials, they might parade their vain insignificance, and no one would notice them; but we ought to make it a serious offence to thus abuse the glorious monogram of our country, and thereby give so apt occasion to foreigners for interpreting the title in a manner more expressive than complimentary."

"Thank you for the hint, papa," said the youngest daughter; "and I give you my firm pledge that 'Minnie Dean' shall be innocent of any chalk or charcoal immortality during our whole journey."

"I should think no lady," remarked Ella, "would be so indiscreet as to parade her name in such a public manner; it is in exceedingly bad taste, if indeed it is not really vulgar."

"I am afraid, my daughter," was the father's reply, "that if the egotistical registers referred to were carefully searched, we should find that the petty ambition of some of our countrywomen is stronger than their sense of womanly modesty. But let us finish our lesson.

"Not far from the 'Sugar Loaf,' on which I met my dangerous experience, a splendid natural bridge is found, called the 'Arched Rock.' It is situated one hundred and forty feet above the lake, and is of very graceful proportions. The erosion of the water has chiseled out a beautiful arch, and left it as a monument of its skill. Like the 'Sugar Loaf,' it is full of crevices and dwarf cedars, and is an object worth making a long pilgrimage to see. It tells in unmistakable language of the mighty changes which have taken place in the surface of the country. The marks of watery influences are distinctly traceable from the top to the bottom of the gulf which it spans, and of course one of two things must be true— either that the waters of the lake were once a hundred and forty feet higher than they are now, or that the whole island has been pushed up correspondingly: the former supposition being the most probable.

"From this sketch it will be seen that God provides by these displays of power for gratifying the eyes as well as for storing up the great essentials of life, and the richness of the materialistic blessing ought not to cause us to lose sight of his ample provision for the more refined pleasures of taste. How often are we exhorted to 'behold the works of God,' to 'see that he is good'! The material wealth of nature ministers to the animal appetite of man, but its grandeur and beauty address themselves to his higher faculties of mind and heart; one feeds his body and warms it, the other inspires his soul and elevates his affections. In looking, therefore, at God's treasures unlocked and placed within our reach, we must not be satisfied in putting the riches into our pockets, but add a larger income to our mind-wealth and heart-wealth.

"With these preparatory lessons, we shall be in some degree better prepared to understand the scenes which will engage our special attention in our contemplated journey, to whose developments we will leave the further study of our Black Diamond."

CHAPTER XI.

OFF FOR THE MINES.

SOME time before daylight on the morning of the intended visit, Minnie Dean was startled from her pleasant dreams by the consciousness that some person was in her room, and was even fumbling with the locks of her hair. Starting up with a suppressed scream, and throwing out her hand, it encountered the turbaned head of the old cook, who affectionately said,

"Dar, dar, honey! it's jes' me. I wants ter put ye in de care of de good Lord. Oh, chile, it's drefful to go way down dar in de darkness. Why, dar's heaps ob folks killed down dar. De stones fall on dem, and de 'splosions kill 'm, and de dreffel pisen go creepin' roun',' and de first ting ye knows, ye's jes' as brack as ole Comfort. Jo Derison, he's bin dar, an' he tole me all 'bout it, an' I couldn't let ye go nohow till I comes an' jes' puts my hans on my precious lam', and tells de bressed Saviour to take good car' ob her and gib her back to de fole."

"Dear, dear, good Comfort," said the tearful child as she laid her head on the loving bosom of the dear old woman, "I do love you so much and thank you for your prayers. I am sure the Lord will hear you on my behalf, and I shall come back to you all safe; but I want you to pray for me daily that I may be a good girl and love the precious Saviour as you do."

"My precious lam'," responded the old cook, laying her hand gently on the curling silken locks of her pet, "I does love de bressed Jesus, but my ole' heart's very naughty sometimes, an' I makes de crooked path, and finds de thorns and de briers, an' sometimes please de eye and pain de heart; but I'se pray for ye all de time since I tote ye in my han', when ye's not bigger dan your little doll-baby. Oh, my chile, I'se live for ye. I'se noting else in de worl' dat please my ole heart. I 'spects yer fadder an' yer mudder, yer sister and Massa Milton, dey's all good an' kin' to me, honey; but, precious chile, I'se nurse ye all yer life, an' when I tinks ob ye or puts my han' on yer head, my ole' heart swell up big, for I jes' totes ye on it; an' if ye don't come back to me, it'll jes' break all to pieces."

"I shall come back to you all safe, Comfort," said the girl, caressing the old woman, "and then I will tell you all about the strange things I may see; but now, Comfort, help me to get all my things ready, for I'm so excited I'll be 'most sure to forget something."

While this affectionate interview was taking place, the Dean household had aroused into general activity, preparing for the early start which they must make to meet the proper train at the station about seven miles off.

Breakfast was despatched, trunks packed, shawls and waterproofs strapped, and then, gathering round the family altar, those who journeyed and those who tarried at home were committed to the gracious keeping of him in whom alone is safety.

Anon the ringing notes of the stage-horn sent the whole household to see the travelers off. Among the rest was the old cook, with her nicely filled traveling lunch-basket, which Mr. Dean took from her hand, at the same time gratifying the old woman by saying,

"Thank you, Comfort; you have put up a bountiful store for us, I see, and I have no doubt but that the quality is equal to the quantity."

"I'se done my bes', Massa Dean, an' hopes dar's 'nough to las' till ye gets to Mong Chong; but take car' of yerse'f, and don't let Miss Minnie get los' in dem dark places. An' young Massa Milton—ye'll hav' ter watch dat boy, he's so ventersom', or ye'll miss him som' whar, sure."

"I think," replied Mr. Dean, "we shall have no mishaps to mar our pleasure; but, Comfort, I want you to take good care of your mistress, and do not allow her to turn the house quite upside down, as I think she has some intention of doing, under the sanction of a general cleaning."

"Do not be alarmed, husband," replied the wife; "I presume when I shall receive back my husband and children that they will be in a much more dilapidated condition than the house, whatever disturbances I may make in its arrangements, and that they will need quite as much renovation."

"Quite likely, my dear—quite likely," was Mr. Dean's playful response; "and so we will say goodbye, in the hope that neither will be so great as to be past a speedy restoration."

After an affectionate embrace, Mr. Dean turned to assist in getting the trunks arranged on the stage, while the children were receiving their farewell kisses from the mother, with many an earnest admonition to be careful of health, limbs, and bundles. Finally, all things were properly adjusted, and with a crack of the whip the stage whirled away on its drive to the station. The last thing heard was the voice of old Comfort, saying,

"Massa Dean, take good care of de chillen when ye's down dar in de darkness."

It was a beautiful morning in mid-summer, still and balmy, yet sweet and elastic, as the air came to the lungs perfumed and fresh from the vigorous growth of the season. The whole feathered choir were in full song, and made the very air tremulous with their music. The landscape melted softly away in the distance, till it touched the high range of eastern hills, above which hung a long pencil-shaped cloud, stretching away dreamy and motionless.

Mrs. Dean watched the retreating vehicle until it passed out of sight at an angle in the road, and then turned to re-enter her quite deserted home, remarking to Comfort, as her eyes lingered for a moment on the beautiful scene of the morning,

"Well, Comfort, they have a most delightful morning for their start."

"Dat's so, Mis' Liz'beth; de good Lord hab gib dem a shinin' mornin', an I hope dey'll bring de sunshine back wid dem. I'se pray for dat all de time, an' I kinder spects de Lord will hear jis what I tole him."

"I am sure he will, Comfort, and my fervent prayers shall go with yours for their safe return."

"Oh, Mis' Liz'beth, what a bressed ting it is dat we can put all our cares on Massa Jesus, and he takes dem all and totes dem away off, an we feel so light an' happy, as do' we nebber hab any trouble!"

"Yes, Comfort, such are his promises, and they are always fulfilled to those who trust in them."

"Ah, Mis' Liz'beth, I does trus' him, an' he's nebber forgot ole Comfort yet, an' so I'm sure he'll jes gib my little lam' back agin, an' dat's all dat keeps de tears from de eyes now."

"Oh, Comfort," said Mrs. Dean, with her eyes suffused, "if you can feel so much attachment for those whom you have only nursed, what must be the yearnings of a mother's heart?"

"Dat's true, Miss Liz'beth; you'se dar mudder, but I'se nus dem chillen, an' rock dem in de cradle, an' carry dem in my bosum, an' I'se a share in dem."

"So you have, Comfort, and I am grateful for the affection you have always shown them, and will try and repay it."

"I wants no pay, Mis' Liz'beth, for I'se already paid. Dey lubs me, an' dat's worf mor'n all tings else."

"So it is, Comfort, and that is just what I meant; I will try to show my love to you as you have ever shown yours to me and mine."

"De Lord bress you! You'se always been kine to me, an' I'se happy wid ye."

"It shall be my care, Comfort, that you continue so." So saying, the two passed into the house to the duties which demanded their attention.

The route of the party which had just left was by way of Philadelphia, Bethlehem, and the Lehigh Gap to Mauch Chunk; then to Scranton, Carbondale, and back by way of Pottsville, down the Schuylkill, home. They were to stop at the various places where they wished to examine the mines or other objects of interest, as circumstances should dictate, making Mauch Chunk the principal point of delay. The reader will not be taxed with any of the incidents occurring while passing over the familiar portions of the route, until the party reaches Slatington, near the Gap, where Mr. Dean wished to spend a day in examining the slate-quarries, explaining to his children their relation to the coal-measures.

Slatington is situated on the Lehigh River but a short distance below the Gap, and takes its name from the chief business of the place, which is the working of the slate-quarries cropping out of the neighboring hills. This business is carried on extensively on both sides of the river, where slates of most excellent quality are quarried and prepared for the market. Abundance of red and black shales and slates are found in all parts of the anthracite regions, most generally of a soft texture easily disintegrated by frost and rain, and forming an excellent soil for grass and grain. But it is only where the older slate is met with—that underlying the coal-beds—that a quality is found adapted to the purposes of roofing. This formation is an interesting study, as well as being valuable for building purposes. It is older than the coal-measures, rich in some of the first forms of life, and, except mica, is the most beautiful illustration of the laminated form of rocks, as it can be split into very thin and perfect sheets, as seen in its commercial form of building-slates, making one of the handsomest and most enduring roofs which can be put upon a house.

As soon as Mr. Dean had arranged matters at his hotel after the arrival of the party, he repaired to one of the quarries, which was but a few rods distant, and began his researches. The men were busily engaged in getting large blocks of slate from the bed and splitting them up into proper thickness, while others, with appropriate machinery, were squaring the edges and laying them away in suitable piles for the market. These matters were soon comprehended, and the party had thus obtained more correct knowledge in a few minutes about the process of fitting roofing-slate, than they could have obtained by reading many pages of the most accurate description.

"Here," said Mr. Dean, stopping near some workmen in the quarry, "you can see the results of the great unlocking process which was the subject of our last conversation. Notice the dip of these slate-beds. You will see at once that if they were followed downward, they would carry us far beyond the base of yonder mountains, under which they do actually sweep, and crop out on the head-waters of the Juniata. Above this slate formation we find the great conglomerate beds, of more than a thousand feet in thickness, forming the immediate flooring of the coal-measures. This conglomerate is seen in mighty drifts of loose boulders slowly creeping down the mountain-sides or crumbling down the deep cuts of the railroads, sometimes in clean-washed piles of stones, or mixed with dirt and gravel. Now let us go down, in imagination, to the position which the undisturbed coal-beds would occupy under the centre of this immense basin, and what a plunge we should have to take into the bowels of the earth! It would be quite a start in the direction of China. But leaving this view of the great basin, let us climb to the top of Summit Hill, and we shall find the Black Diamond cropping out there and glistening in its sides, tilted in every possible form of disturbance. What arm but that of Omnipotence could do this? 'He putteth forth his hand upon the rocks; he overturneth the mountains by the roots.' Notice that little notch yonder in the distant mountains. That is the Lehigh Water Gap, one of the massive doors which the divine Hand threw open when it fashioned these hills to let the prisoned waters flow out, and admit us into the great treasure-house which he had created among the mountains beyond. Looking at that, we may continue the language of Job, and say, 'He cutteth out rivers among the rocks, and his eye seeth every precious thing.' But let us examine this slate a little more carefully. It is evidently formed out of the erosions of the older rocks; the ground-up lava and débris from the action of the waves were deposited in the great basins slowly and without much disturbance. This was indurated, and perhaps, as each successive tide swept along, a new and thin deposit was left on the face of the last, this being sufficiently hardened to mark the distinct layers. By and by, as the crust of the earth was thickened by the succeeding epochs, the pressure to which it was subjected, combined with some chemical action, compressed the plastic mass into its stony compactness, yet preserved its lamina. The old, primitive way of making paper will furnish us with an apt illustration. This was formerly done exclusively by hand. The pasty mass of ground rags was mixed, and then spread sheet by sheet over broad pieces of felt, and laid one upon another until a huge pile was formed. When these sheets were dry enough, they were placed under the power of a strong screw-press, and compressed into the utmost thinness and density. Now, take one of these piles of green paper and tilt up one edge or compress the sides laterally, and we should have formations analogous to those beds of slate. As that paper would be firmest and best which was subjected to the greatest pressure, so the best slates are those which are quarried from the oldest and deepest beds, where they have endured the greatest weight of the superincumbent earth, and been subjected longer and more thoroughly to the influence of heat and chemical action.

"You will notice that these slate rocks are not deposited with continuous unbroken strata, but are intersected by crevices called cleavage—that is, they not only split into laminæ, but transversely along their seams, which enables the quarrymen to remove the masses with much greater ease, and makes them more susceptible of being easily worked up into merchantable tiles."

"Father," said Milton, "I'm so glad you stopped here, though I was sorry at first, I am so anxious to see Mauch Chunk, for I've learned so much that I did not know before. I knew that slate was quarried out of the ground, and that was all I knew about the matter; but now I think I have a clear idea of the subject."

"You must restrain your anxiety to push ahead, my son, or you will greatly mar the pleasure of your journey. When we have anything to see or learn, let us take all the time necessary to make the occasion profitable. 'More haste, less speed,' will apply to journeys and sightseeing as well as to many other affairs of life."

"I'm sure I'm not in a hurry," said Ella, "for the scenery here is so grand I could spend days in viewing it as well as the slate-beds."

"Have some pretzels? Da isch right fresh and goot," just then sounded in the ears of the party as an old German woman held out the well-known Pennsylvania product.

"Ha, ha! isn't that rather going from the sublime to the ridiculous?" inquired Minnie—"from grand mountains to a penny pretzel; and as Ella is feeding on the mountain, I will take the smaller eatable, as I have often wondered what a pretzel was."

"Pretzels are goot, mein fräulein," said the old woman, "and I makes dem meinself; and here's some nice 'smearcase,' only tree cent abiece," holding out a small cake of something looking like boiled rice.

"Smearcase!" ejaculated Milton; "what in the world is that, father? Is it something to eat?"

"Someding to eat?" said the old woman, somewhat snappishly; "to be sure it's someding to eat, and good enough for you or de young ladies; I makes him meinself—Frau Hunsucker."

"Yes, yes, my good woman," said Mr. Dean; "my son does not understand what you mean. Your smearcase we call cottage cheese, and we are not in want of any just now, but we will take a few of your pretzels, as my children have never tasted any and wish to try them."

"Ja, mynheer, da is goot," said the old woman, at the same time handing Milton a couple of the pretzels, who had no sooner tasted one than he spit it from his mouth, exclaiming,

"Bah! if any one calls that good, he must have a queer taste. Why, it's as hard as a stick and salt as a mackerel."

"A pretzel is not the most elegant article of diet," said Mr. Dean, "but it is very highly esteemed by the old German families of Pennsylvania, and it is one of the coveted accomplishments of these thrifty housewives to make a good pretzel, crisp, brown, and not too salt. But we did not stop here to discuss the qualities of pretzels, so let us finish our inspection of the slate-quarries."

The party spent the remainder of the day in their researches, and became pretty thoroughly acquainted with the whole details of the slate formations of the neighborhood and the state of the trade, and finally returned to the hotel delighted with their afternoon's ramble.

Early the next morning the travelers were again on the cars, and were soon nearing the gap in the mountains which they had noticed the day before in the distance. When passing round the graceful curve, just as they were about to enter the pass, Mr. Dean called the attention of his children to the grandeur of the picture.

"Look!" said he; "there is one of the great doors which God unlocked leading into his treasure-house of Black Diamonds. When we pass through this grand entrance, we shall be ushered into one of the most attractive regions in the whole country. It is also rich in coal, and the section where the anthracite variety was first discovered. From this point to Mauch Chunk, and far above that place, the river Lehigh passes through one vast cañon, its waters tumbling in a succession of beautiful cascades and rapids. High rocks and jutting crags sometimes hang over the track of the road, seemingly ready at the least disturbance to topple over on the trains sweeping beneath them. Now and then little glens cut their way up the mountain sides, and minute cataracts send a glistening veil of tributary waters to the Lehigh. Now feast your eyes," he continued, "for every rod between this and Mauch Chunk is a picture worth coming the whole distance to look at."

It needed no admonition to fix the attention of Milton and his sisters on the grand scenery lying between the Lehigh Gap and Mauch Chunk; but their enthusiasm culminated as they turned the last curve in the mountain just before reaching the latter place. Ella fairly clapped her hands in her ecstasy of delight; and when the train stopped before the Mansion House, she hardly knew whether she was in the flesh or out of it, and it required two or three admonitions of Mr. Dean before she was really aware that the train had stopped and she was in Mauch Chunk.

Mr. Dean had visited the place several times, and was well known at the Mansion House, seen at the left hand, near the end of the bridge, and was a particular friend of the colored porter of the hotel, one of the noted characters of the place. (Fig. 12.) No sooner, therefore, had the party alighted, than he was greeted in the warmest manner by his colored friend:

"Why, Massa Dean, is dis you? I'se mighty glad to see you; an' de ladies, bless us! how s'lubrous dey looks! Walk right into de parlor! I'se tend to de trunks, and fotch'm d'eckly." Then he uttered his

Black Diamonds. Mauch Chunk. Page 164.

stereotyped cry, "Twenty minutes for dinnah;" "Step dis way, gemmen;" "Heah's de dinin'-room;" and "All right," addressed to the conductor of the train when all the passengers had passed into the hotel.

FIG. 12.—*The Porter.*

Mr. Dean and his children were soon delightfully settled in a couple of communicating rooms, directly facing Bear Mountain, with a beautiful sweep up the river from the verandah, while its waters were leaping and foaming below them. Here they sat during the delightful evening, watching the rich floods of moonlight that came down over the tops of the mountains and touched the glimmering waters, and the long coal-trains as one after another they passed up and down the river. They were especially interested in counting the number of cars in the different trains, and found them to vary from seventy-five to two hundred. Often one would form a curve entirely around Bear Mountain, so that the engine would be on one side and the caboose car, attached to the rear, quite out of sight on the other. But what astonished them most was that one of these trains passed on an average every two minutes, night and day. It gave them a new conception of the mighty traffic in Black Diamonds. It was thus seen that several hundred trains and many thousand cars, half of them loaded for the market, passed every day. But this was not all. Just above the dam forming the lockage of the canal, they saw a whole fleet of boats taking in coal at the coal-slides at the foot of Mount Pisgah. When their load was completed, they dropped through the canal lock just opposite the hotel, and pursued their way to the market, adding very largely to the daily exportation.

"Well, father," said Milton, after watching this busy scene for hours and making his calculations,

"I'm paid for my journey if I should go home to-morrow. I begin to have some idea of the worth of the Black Diamond, and why God stored away such an abundance of it. If they dig out coal in such vast quantities as we have seen pass since we came here, it seems to me they must exhaust the mines before long."

"Not much fear of that, my son; God's storehouses are not so easily exhausted. But the scene before us is grand both in its natural surroundings and as exhibiting the energy of man's industries and inventions for supplying the great wants of the world. Let us not, however, weary our minds by overtaxing them with too many wonders at once; so happy dreams for the night, and a Switchback ride in the morning."

"Here, papa," said Minnie, "is a good long kiss for our day's pleasure."

"And two of them from me," added Ella.

"Thank you, daughters; and so good-night!"

CHAPTER XII.

AROUND THE SWITCHBACK.

IT was a long time after the young folks had retired before sleep visited their eyes. The sharp melody of the dancing waters just under their window, the continued blare of locomotive whistles, and the ceaseless rumble of cars, kept them awake. Milton for some time kept up a continual journey to and from his window, as train after train swept its sinuous length around the curve of Bear Mountain or came from the dark shadows of the gorge above. He would curiously watch the head-lights of the engines, swelling from the dimensions of a firefly when first seen till they burst into the full glare of a furnace, and then receding again, until finally lost in the distance or suddenly hidden by a curve in the road. The scene was so different from the usually quiet surroundings of Willow Brook it was very difficult to realize that a single day's ride had produced it. But finally

"Tired Nature's sweet restorer, balmy sleep,"

came to their relief, and mountains, coal, and cars were alike forgotten in its sweet embraces.

Morning comes by the clock as early at Mauch Chunk as at any other place of the same latitude, but by reason of its surroundings the rising of the sun on its inhabitants is postponed for an hour or two later, with a corresponding hastening of the hour of setting. It required, therefore, the kind offices of the porter to arouse the party next morning, that they might be in readiness for the early train around the Switchback—a charge which he had received from Mr. Dean the evening before. Accordingly, at the proper time his knock came and his cheerful voice was heard calling out,

"Massa Dean, de sun am up in odder places, but he's kinder forget heself heah; so you mus' rouse de young ladies if dey wants dar breakfas' befor' dey p'rambulate roun' de Switchback."

"Thank you, thank you!" was Mr. Dean's reply; "we will be ready in due time."

Soon after, the whole party were busy with their morning toilette, but the young people spent much more time at their windows than before their glasses, the scene was so unusual and wild in the gray mist of the early morning. Bear Mountain was wrapt in a cold gray mantle, whose skirts swept down toward the gap, while the northern range was canopied in a like garment. A half dozen or more locomotives, resting, as it were, from their night's struggles among the mountain grades, were blowing off huge columns of vapor, which, in the pulseless air, ascended to the misty ocean hanging over the place, their tops spreading out into fantastic capitals as they touched the cloud, as though intended to support this aërial architecture. And how that chorus of whistles echoed and re-echoed among the mountains, back and forth, as though weaving a texture of voices above to veil the slumbering town! The scene was weird and startling, and might have called a devotee of Fashion from the altar of her devotions. Ella stood so absorbed as to be almost powerless as she said to her sister,

"Isn't it grand, Minnie? Indeed, I'd rather have sat up all night than have missed the sight, and now feel inclined to go without my breakfast, that I may see the vision to the last."

"Yes, sister," replied Minnie, "it's sublime, no doubt, but just now you had better let mountains and clouds alone, and get dressed."

"Oh, Min, you are so horribly prosaic!" said her sister. "How can you think of dress or anything, with such a scene before you?"

"That may be," was the reply; "but just now I confess to a great admiration for beefsteaks and coffee, and will take the mountains as a dessert when they can be more easily digested, and had rather get the snarls out of my own hair than watch the mists curling around the mountain-heads."

"Folks would think," said Ella, "should they hear you talk, that you belong to the race of wild animals that give a name to the opposite mountain— unless, perhaps, I do them injustice by the comparison, for they must have had some admiration for the scene, or they would not have so lingered around the place as to identify their name with it."

"Well, I guess that's so, sister," was the quizzical response, "for I do feel a little 'bearish' in my appetite this morning, and so you had better hurry, or I may take a savage notion to try my teeth on something human before I reach the breakfast-table."

Just then the father's rap was heard on the door, while he called out,

"Come, come, daughters! we are ready for breakfast, and have not much time to lose."

This hurried the girls in their remaining preparations, and they were soon after seated around the table enjoying their morning repast, during which Mr. Dean informed the children that he intended to spend the day in simply making the excursion around the Switchback road and a general survey of the scenery, leaving for another day a more careful inspection of the mines; hence they would need no special preparations.

Not long after breakfast was finished, the voice of the porter was heard crying out,

"All aboard, gemmen; de omnibus for de Switchback am at de do'r."

Leaving the hotel, there is a short drive up the street directly on the banks of the river, then a sudden turn to the left into the main thoroughfare of the place, which passes up through a mere notch between the mountains, so narrow as simply to allow the row of buildings which face on the street. Above these, on both sides, rise several terraces one above the other, so steep that the inhabitants above can throw stones into the chimneys of their neighbors in the next lower tiers.

The main street is followed but a short distance before a turn to the right begins the steep and narrow ascent to upper Mauch Chunk, situated immediately at the foot of Mount Pisgah. The road is constructed by digging into the mountain side and throwing out the dirt, making a roadway barely wide enough for the passing of two wagons, some parts of which have no sort of wall or railing as a protection. To persons sitting on the lower or valley side of the omnibus it has an unpleasantly suggestive look. As the ascent is slowly made the passengers thus seated have a view almost directly down the chimneys of the houses situated on the terraces below them. Away down yonder is the jail. Its massive stone walls are proof against all of its unfortunate inmates who may attempt to escape by climbing out, but an unlucky turn of two or three feet would seemingly land the omnibus and all of its passengers in it, instead of taking them to the foot of Mount Pisgah, for which they started.

Minnie happened to have a seat on this side of the vehicle, and the trial was quite enough for even her strong nerves. She looked and shuddered, and finally said,

"Oh, papa, I hope I may never have to go to jail; but if I must do so, I prefer to go in the legitimate way, rather than be tumbled through the top of its chimney, of which there seems a great probability just now."

"Let us get out and walk," said the nervous and timid Ella. "I'm sure we shall tumble over the bank before we get to the top, and, like sister, I don't want to tumble into prison, even if I must go there."

"Don't be alarmed, miss," said one of the omnibus drivers, who happened to be a passenger that morning; "we tried that once, and they wouldn't take us in. They'll accommodate any legitimate house-breaker, but coming down chimney they said was not commitable burglary."

The laughter which followed this consoling assurance of the driver was not exactly appreciated by the half-frightened girls, who were only relieved from their anxiety when the omnibus turned to the right and entered the main street of the upper town. They rode about half a mile through the place, and passed by the beautiful cemetery, which is situated on a point of land jutting out into a handsome plateau; then they took another sharp turn to the left and a short run down hill; finally the party were landed without any disaster at the foot of the grand inclined plane by which ascent is made to the highest point of Mount Pisgah. A single look at this formidable superstructure set the girls once more into a nervous quaking.

"Oh, father," said Ella, "we are not going up that terrible place, are we?"

"That is the beginning of our route to the Switch-back, my daughter; and though it has rather a fearful look, there is no danger. The wire cable that will draw us up will scarcely feel our weight, after taking up long trains of coal-cars; besides, look down into these holes at the foot of the plain, and you will see the 'safety cars.' They are so adjusted as to stop the train anywhere on the plane at the least

Black Diamonds. Page 175.
Inclined Plane to Mt. Pisgah.

backward movement; so if the rope should break, there would no harm result. In all the years during which this road has been used no serious accident has occurred; so you must not let your groundless fears mar the pleasure of the trip."

Thus in some measure assured, the girls nerved themselves for the ascent. If Milton felt any timidity, he was successful in concealing it, and was jubilant in his delight.

This grand plane is twenty-three hundred and twenty-two feet in length, with a direct elevation of six hundred and sixty-four feet, or a rise of one foot in three. It has a double track, with two stationary engines located on the top of the mountain, where the two smoke-stacks can be seen. For passengers, open and closed cars are used, as the excursionists choose, the former being far preferable for enjoying the magnificent scenery along the road; and as there are no sparks or dust, they are quite as comfortable also.

The road was at first, what its name imports, a switchback—that is, so constructed as to switch itself from one plane to another—but now it is a simple gravity road. It was at first constructed for the coal-trade, and made the whole circuit of the mines, a distance of some twenty-five miles, but is now used exclusively for excursionists, and terminates at Summit Hill, making only about half the original distance.

When a couple of cars were ready, Mr. Dean chose the open one, it being in the rear also, giving the best facilities for admiring the scenery as they went up the plane. When all were ready, the conductor pulled a wire which hung by a post and was seen stretching up the mountain like a telegraph wire, connecting with the engineer's bell at the summit, and instantly the cars began to move, passing over the short level between the station and the foot of the plane, and then, suddenly tilting up at a sharp angle, began to climb the mountain. Although expected, yet when it came there was a suppressed scream, and the girls clung convulsively to the arms of the father as they sat on each side of him, Minnie being toward the foot of the ascent. Up, up, they mount, while the river and town seem to be sinking into the ground, and Bear Mountain grows pigmy in dimensions as the pinnacles of other ranges shoot up beyond, as though just evoked from the earth's bosom by the touch of a magician's wand.

Still up they mount; and the car in which Mr. Dean and his children were seated being in the rear, the cable by which they were drawn up was out of sight, making it seem to them as though they were fairly suspended over the receding town lying so far below them. It was too much for the timid Ella, who clutched her father's arm most frantically as she cried out,

"Oh, father, we shall fall out! I know we shall! Please stop the car and let us get out."

"Come, come, my daughter," said Mr. Dean, "you are unduly alarmed; there is really no danger; besides, there would be more risk to attempt to get out here than to go on."

Minnie really had to hold fast to her father to prevent sliding out of the rear of the car. Having nerved herself for the occasion, she was wholly engrossed with the grand prospect, and sat looking down the plane, watching the rapid and wonderful transformations which every rod of the ascension brought to view, to which she in vain tried to call the attention of the frightened sister.

"Why, Ella, look," said she, "and don't spoil your ride by being so foolish. We're not half so heavy as the train of coal-cars which just passed us, and they didn't break the rope."

"Who's afraid?" shouted Milton. "Why, it's just as good as going up in a balloon," at the same time jumping up to show his bravery, only to find himself the next moment thrown halfway down the car, and barely saved from going its whole length, or possibly quite out at the rear, by the quick and strong

M

grasp of his father. He was restored to his seat quite chapfallen.

"Youngster," said the conductor, "if you don't want a worse collapse than that, you had better keep your seat, or you may find yourself at upper Mauch Chunk, instead of on the top of Pisgah."

By the time the train was two-thirds of the way up all had become so assured that they began to drink in the grand panorama that was spreading out wider and wider below them; and when with a jerk and a tilt forward the car shot into the station-house on the summit, they were in the wildest mood of wonder and delight. From that elevated position, look in whatever direction they might, the scenery was grand beyond description. By special request the train was delayed for half an hour, that the party might walk out on the points of the mountain and the trestle-work connecting it with the range beyond, to enjoy the magnificence of the landscapes spread out below and beyond them. Very naturally, the first look was at the town, now lying near a thousand feet below. Far in the distance, on looking south, the Lehigh Gap was seen, through which they had passed on the day before; while a glance down the notch, up which they had passed in the omnibus, showed the little town nestled in its deep cradle, with Bear Mountain just across the river, which was now

Mauch Chunk, from Mt. Pisgah.

dwindled into a little bow of glistening silver. Over the tops of the trees beneath which is situated the Mansion House they could see the trains circling round the graceful curves of the railroads, with the mountains hanging almost perpendicularly over them. Looking northward, the scene was equally enchanting. Indeed, from that highest point the eye can turn in no direction but it is greeted with a vision that holds it spellbound. Amid such surroundings the coveted half hour was soon spent, and it was with regret that the conductor's cry was heard: "All aboard for the Switchback!" Once more seated in the little open car, it began mysteriously to move over the light trestle-work and follow the windings of the range of mountains beyond, which leads out to Summit Hill and the coal-mines. The power that moves the traveler around the Switchback road is simply that of gravity. Beginning at the highest point at Mount Pisgah, the grade is between ninety and a hundred feet to the mile, and quite sufficient to give a good speed to the cars, which are kept under perfect control by the brakesman, who sits in front with his hand on the lever, ever ready to check any undue speed or stop the train at pleasure. On and on swept the self-moving train, while the rocks on one side grew higher and higher, and on the other frequent and enchanting glimpses of the valley below and of the opposite range of mountains were caught through the openings of the luxuriant foliage.

With all sense of danger gone, the ride was enjoyed with unalloyed pleasure, until the train brought up at the foot of Mount Jefferson, six miles distant. Here another plane awaited their ascent; but familiarized by their experience at Pisgah, the whole party enjoyed the trip up the steep road, though the timid Ella could not look downward without a shudder of dizziness.

"Here," said Mr. Dean as they tilted over on to the summit, "is the highest point above tidewater in this vicinity, being about sixteen hundred and thirty-five feet; and yonder," at the same time pointing to a range of hills, "is Summit Hill, where the way into the vast treasure-house of Black Diamonds was first discovered, and where they are yet obtained in the largest quantities."

Again the unseen engineer started the cars, and after a few minutes' ride the mining town of Summit Hill was entered, generally the terminus of the Switchback ride; but as Mr. Dean wished to make the round trip through the working mines, they kept their seats, and were soon carried into the Panther Creek Valley. Here on every side were the openings into the mines, great hills of coal-dirt, large coal-breakers in full operation, coal-cars, filled and empty, miners' houses, wives, and children, and miners themselves, many of them black in the face as the lumps of coal that were scattered all about. Troops of coal-smutted children crowded round the cars with various minerals and pieces of coal carved into miniature books, boots, or other forms, for sale. The scene was so unique that Minnie said,

"Comfort was pretty near right when she said there were many curious creatures down in those dark places; but they don't seem to come in a very spiritual form, though they certainly are 'black spirits and gray,' if they do belong to the misty sisterhood."

"I rather guess their fondness for money," said the father, "too clearly identifies them with flesh and blood; but we shall have a good chance to determine to what race they belong when we visit the mines for the purpose of careful inspection, and so we will let them pass for to-day."

Again the cars moved, taking them through many similar scenes and up three other smaller planes, now dispensed with, and anon they found themselves back again at the Summit Hill station, ready for the long stretch back to Mauch Chunk. This passage is much lower down on the mountain, but is most delightful, the last few miles being along a little creek abounding in beautiful miniature cascades and shady pools.

> "Now purling round the sunken rocks,
> Or misty jewels flinging,
> Where gambol dace and speckled trout,
> As down the cascade springing."

The party finally landed at upper Mauch Chunk, and were back at the Mansion House in time for a seasonable dinner, which they enjoyed with the keen appetite which the forenoon's ride and the deep quaffing of the bracing mountain air had given them.

CHAPTER XIII.

AT THE MINES.

AFTER dinner and some attention to the toilet, Milton and his sisters resorted to the verandah of the hotel, from which one can obtain a very extended view of the splendid scenery and busy life of Mauch Chunk. Before them was a picture conceived in one of Nature's grandest inspirations, in which are inwrought the boldest outlines with the finest touches of light and shade, leaving no semblance of monotony in any of its accessories. In harmony with these sublime efforts of Nature, the works of man coming within the same range of view approach the sublime, sweeping from the ever-rattling coal-chutes on the river to the massive engines on the top of Pisgah.

On both sides of the river the mountains have been graded and girded with the iron rails, over which is a continual rush of the immense and ponderous coal-trains, interspersed with the splendid passenger cars which drop their loads of curious travelers many times a day. The canal-boats lie in fleets above the locks, through which a constant succession of them is passing, each with its trio of sober-looking mules and its exceedingly noisy driver. These are the sights that meet the eye at every point, while the ears are astonished by an equally wondrous combination of sounds. The harsh rattle of the coal-chutes, screaming of locomotive whistles, rush and rumble of car-wheels, bumping and jerking of colliding cars, blending with the boatman's horn and the ceaseless splash of the turbulent Lehigh,—all make up a grand chorus as a befitting anthem to the surroundings. Add to this the bustle of an exceedingly busy place, which Nature has cramped into the closest possible limits, and perhaps there is scarcely another scene of equal and startling variety to be found.

Tediousness will seldom visit persons looking at this magnificent panorama, however long they may continue the contemplation. Though so contracted in its range, it is a vast kaleidoscope whose endless and startling changes hold the mind with unflagging interest.

After a long enjoyment of the scenes just described, and when the sun had become hidden behind the brow of the mountain in the rear of the hotel, in company with their father, the children made their way up to the well-known Prospect Rock, from which a wider and more impressive view can be had of the grand combination of landscape and enterprise already described, and which had held them so long on the verandah. With this indulgence that eventful day of their lives was closed, and evening found them much more disposed to yield to the soothing embraces of slumber than they had been on the previous night, and which the father had admonished them would be necessary as a preparation for the severe tax which would be made on their strength the coming day.

When morning returned and breakfast had been enjoyed, suitable preparations were made for the climbing of hills and creeping through mines, and then they started for another ride on the Switchback as far as Summit Hill, where the inspection of the mines was to begin.

With their previous day's experience, the timidity which had so marred the pleasure of the first ascent of Mount Pisgah was quite removed, and it was enjoyed with the utmost exhilaration, as was the whole ride until they landed at their destination.

The first object to be inspected was the great open quarry where Philip Gunther first discovered the Black Diamond, in 1791. He was a poor hunter and trapper who had settled among the mountains, where he could obtain an abundance of game. But on this occasion he had been wholly unsuccessful, and was going home through a cold, drizzling rain, moodily brooding over the wants of a hungry family. In his progress he chanced to stumble over a black stone, which was exposed where a tree had been blown down; and having heard that coal was supposed to be hidden in the mountains near there, he suspected that this might be a specimen of the treasure, and selected a piece for examination, when his surmises proved to be correct. Like many others, however, who have discovered some great resource of human wealth, poor Gunther was about as successful in his coal speculation as he had been in that day's hunting.

As the party found the place, it was an open, abandoned quarry of several acres in extent; but when first discovered, it was a marvelous instance of the great upheavals which brought the treasures of coal from their deep foundations to this most accessible position. When the party had entered the excavation, Mr. Dean said,

"Here once stood, not the 'Mountain of Light,' as the largest known lump of pure carbon, the great East India diamond, was called, in admiration of its size and brilliancy, but the greatest known mountain of 'Black Diamonds.' The world as yet has not found its equal, either in position or richness. When discovered, it was a single vein of coal of the enormous thickness of seventy feet, tilted up above the surrounding surface, and as easily quarried as a common ledge of rocks. Up to 1847, when it was finally abandoned, more than two million tons of coal were taken from this rich quarry. But let us pass to an adjoining opening, where the rocks and dirt have

FIG. 13.—*Outcrop of Coal and Deep Chasm.*

fallen into the workings below, and we shall be enabled to see the shapings of the outcrop."

"Why, father," asked Ella, "you don't mean to say that there are mines right under our very feet?"

"Just come over here," replied the father as they approached a clift, down which, at a sharp dip, a thick vein of coal was seen cropping out. "Now look down this opening."

They beheld a deep chasm which had been formed some time before by the crust caving in and swallowing up quite a large section of the railroad track and other surroundings.

"Oh, father," exclaimed the alarmed girl, "let us go away; perhaps it might cave in again."

"Such an event may certainly happen," replied the father, "but is not likely to occur from the additional pressure of our weight. These casualties generally follow heavy falls of rain, or result from the powerful leverage of freezing and sudden thawing. We shall see many deep basins formed in this way by the caving in of mines, which sometimes have swallowed up the dwellings of the poor miners. At Hyde Park, opposite Scranton, the line of the main street is cracked in this way, seriously damaging several buildings, including a church and a hotel."

"Indeed," said Minnie, "I wouldn't care to live in such a place, where I might be tumbled into a coal-mine without a moment's warning."

"I think I should rather prefer the safer position of 'Cosy Cottage' at Willow Brook," replied the father, "though we cannot get our coals quite so easily."

"I think," responded Milton, "that is getting them rather too easily, to be tumbled headlong into the native mines after them, and sometimes taking your stove along with you, to save the trouble of bringing them up."

After these statements, notwithstanding the assurances of safety, Ella and Minnie both were quite ready to leave the place where such an event had once occurred, Minnie remarking that she had no desire to take a ride on an avalanche of coal.

Turning from this scene, the enormous mountains of coal-dust heaped up in several directions arrested the special attention of the whole party, one of which, overlooking Panther Creek valley, has a slope of some fifteen hundred feet, from the top of which is had a view but little less grand than that from the top of Mount Pisgah. These huge heaps are a great drawback to the mines and a sad disfigurement to some of the towns in the vicinity, as at Scranton and Hyde Park, and many efforts have been made to utilize the dust, but none have so far succeeded as to make it profitable. In some places it has been successfully used for grading railroad tracks, for which it seems admirably adapted.

The next point of interest was the burning mine.

This mine took fire in 1832, and has been burning ever since, though thousands of dollars and all manner of inventions have been used in attempts to extinguish it. There is no appearance of flame or smoke, but the heat at times is intense and the gas stifling. It is Vesuvius on a small scale. The rocks are baked and turned to every shade of color, as they are in a lime-kiln; and as the strata of coal below are entirely burned away, leaving no supports, they are tilted and heaped in every possible position, with all the interstices filled with ashes and scoriæ. This mine will probably never be extinguished until it goes out from want of materials of combustion. Another mine in the same vicinity, which was more recently ignited, has been subdued by forcing into it a vast volume of carbonic acid gas. As this operation was in progress when Mr. Dean visited the place, he took occasion to impress on the minds of his children a portion of the lesson which he had formerly given touching the agencies God had used in subduing the great primal conflagration.

"Here," said he as they stood watching the operation, "you see a fine illustration of the fact which I named to you in one of our early conversations about the extinguishment of the universal flame that once held our globe in its embraces— that a danger, under the divine control, often produces its own antidote. Carbonic acid gas is the great result of all combustion; but when thus produced, it begins a relentless war on its own parentage. Not even water itself is more intense in its antagonism, nor so effectual in its conflicts. Water is more dense, and immediately seeks the lowest possible level, and only conquers the flames that may be in or below this plane; but the gas can be forced into jets and eddies all through the windings and crevices of the mine, above as well as below, and wherever it goes it leaves but a blackened skeleton behind it. The only contingency of success is a volume of gas of sufficient magnitude and so applied as to be brought directly in contact with the flames. These latter results are nearly secured in the case of the mine we are now considering; hence complete success is fully anticipated, and this mine will be saved from the destructive element which has so long been devouring its more unfortunate neighbor. Mankind have been slow in availing themselves of God's great fire extinguisher, for it has only been within a few years that this gas has been used for the purpose of putting out fires, and even now the effort can be regarded as little more than an experiment."

"I did not fully understand the matter when you first explained it to us," said Milton, "but I think I now comprehend it, and it is wonderful indeed. Just think how strange it is!—an element the most visible and fierce of all things to be so easily subdued by an invisible foe of its own creating. We could hardly believe it possible if we did not see the effect so directly follow the cause."

"Yes, it is wonderful, my son, but not more so than are all of God's works and ways when sought out. In wisdom he has made them all, and his divine superintendency is always seen, either in the direct results or the influence which is exerted on other agencies. 'No man liveth to himself,' nor is there anything in all the range of nature absolutely separate and independent, and this fact most marvelously shows the presence and power of God in the works of creation, for none but an omnipotent being could thus adjust the relations of matter and make of an infinite variety one grand unity."

After spending sufficient time in the vicinity of the burning mines, admiring the grand scenery and learning all they could of the history of the coal-formations so wonderfully placed within reach, they once more took the Switchback cars and passed down into Panther Creek valley, to make the round of the working mines. While passing near the mouth of one of the "drifts," a party of pitmen were just coming out to take their nooning in the open air, and paused to watch the passing train. Their faces were blackened, clothes begrimed, and on their hats little lamps were suspended, some of them still burning. (Fig. 14.) Minnie was the first to notice them, and cried out,

FIG. 14.—*Group of Miners.*

"Oh, father, see what a funny-looking set of men! Are they black men?"

"Well, as they now appear, my daughter, they certainly belong rather to that order; but I think a little soap and water will most likely identify them with the white race."

"Why, Min," said the brother, "how dull you are! Don't you know they are miners? for there on their hats are the little lamps that father told us about."

"Yes, my children," said Mr. Dean, "they are the men who go into the deep and dangerous storehouse of the Black Diamond and bring out the treasure for our use; and though so uncomely now, we ought to do them honor for their service. The life of a miner is one of severe toil and danger, of which we shall have abundant evidence before we get through with our ramblings in the coal regions. Near one-third of his allotted days are spent in the bowels of the earth—a kind of living tomb—often bent and cramped in position, breathing dust and poisonous gases, exposed to premature explosions from blasting and 'fire-damp,' and unconscious how soon the crumbling rocks overhead or the breaking in of the subterranean flood-gates may convert the living tomb into the sepulchre of death. As we sit by our cheerful grates, heaped with glowing anthracite, safe and comfortable, let us remember the toil and dangers which have been incurred by the poor miners to secure us these enjoyments."

"Indeed, father," said Ella, "I'm sure I shall always think of them with kind and grateful feelings hereafter, for their lives must be hard and comparatively pleasureless. What a pity that our comforts cost them so much!"

"Your first impression is true, my daughter; all mining operations involve the severest toil, but the operator need not therefore be without resources of true and rich enjoyment. I have some facts to detail to you, when we shall have a proper opportunity, to show that the roughness of the employment does not necessarily destroy refinement of feeling and nobleness of character; and I could name several distinguished men who have gone from the darkness of these mines to give light to the world of science, law, and the ministry. But we are now at Number Eight mine and breaker, where I propose to make our first underground excursion. So we will bid good-bye to the Switchback for the present, and take our lunch, and then for a trip into the dark opening that you see yonder, which is the 'drift' into the mine. It is a dark, drippy passage, but I think we can make arrangements for a ride in one of the mule-cars which bring out the coal to the breaker, and so we shall be saved from most of the disagreeableness of the journey. But now let us see what we have in our basket."

CHAPTER XIV.

A TRIP UNDER GROUND.

AFTER a hearty enjoyment of the contents of their lunch-basket, Mr. Dean sought the overseer to obtain permission to enter the mines and a guide to accompany them. On making known his wishes, and stating that his special object was a somewhat careful study of the mines and the manner of preparing coal for the market, the desired permission was readily given.

"Certainly, Mr. Dean," was the reply of the gentlemanly superintendent; "you can examine our mines, and we will furnish you with all possible facilities, though your daughters will find it rather rough traveling. As for a guide, we can give you one of the most experienced and trusty miners in our employment. He knows all about the practical working of the mines, in which he has been employed from his earliest boyhood." Saying this, the superintendent turned to a group of pitmen just ready to enter the mines, and called one from the number, when a tall, muscular, and elderly man stepped forth, with his pick in his hand and lamp burning on his hat. (Fig. 15.) Though in the coarse garb

Fig. 15.—*The Old Pitman.*

of the working miner, there was an intelligent and kindly expression in the old man's countenance that at once gave him favor in the eyes of the party about to be confided to his care, and placed them on good terms. Especially was this the case when the old miner learned that Mr. Dean was a member of the same religious brotherhood as himself.

"Well, my friend," said Mr. Dean, on being introduced, "do you think you can take us safely through the mines this afternoon?"

"I trust so, sir," was the reply; "I've worked in the mines since I was a dozen years old, and the Lord has brought me safe through many disasters, some of which were enough to make a man dread to even enter a mine again. Ah, sir, I've seen scores of companions fall before the dreaded gas, or burnt and torn by explosions, and have gone down more than once in the very face of death to rescue my fellow-workmen. But I had the blessed promise, and that I kept repeating to myself when facing the danger: 'Yea, though I walk through the valley of the shadow of death, I will fear no evil, for thy rod and thy staff they comfort me.' But, sir, don't fear; there's no danger to be apprehended where I shall lead you, except what may befall us daily."

This was said, as the old man saw that his detail of disasters was rather untimely as a preparation for strangers to enter where such things had occurred.

"Thank you," was the assuring reply of Mr. Dean; "I am quite willing to follow your lead, and desire to become your pupil for the day, for it is our wish to learn all we can of practical mining."

"I don't pretend to much learning, sir," was the

old man's rejoinder, "but I think it is not vain boasting when I say that few men know more about working coal-mines than I do, and it will give me great pleasure to explain all the operations to you."

"Then," said Mr. Dean, "we will commence just as you would—get into the mine first, and follow the process until it leads us out again."

"That's just what I was going to suggest," replied the miner, "as most natural, if you want to remember much about what you see. But as you have the young ladies with you, I will have a seat fixed in one of the pit cars, if they are not afraid of a little coal-dirt, and they can ride into the mines as far as the mules go."

"Oh, no, no," said Ella; "we expect to get blackened a little, so you need not be anxious about us."

"Well, then," said the old man, "pardon me for a few moments, and I will have all things ready for our excursion."

"Isn't he a nice old man?" said Minnie; "and I shall not be at all afraid to go with him."

"I guess we shall see a rather mischievous face getting long and sober," replied Milton, "when we are tumbling around in the mine."

"Well, that may be, brother, but I don't think it will get much whiter, judging from the condition of those who have made the experiment."

The old man was gone but a short time, and then returned, announcing that all things were ready for the start. After walking a short distance from the office, they approached a large opening in the side of the mountain framed up with wood, before which were seated a number of miners. (Fig. 16.) The guide pointed to the opening, and said,

FIG. 16.—*Entrance to Coal Drift.*

"This is what we call a 'drift' or 'water level,' and is the usual manner of entering a mine when the coal lies above the watercourses in the neighborhood. It is comparatively cheap and easy working the mines when we can thus enter them. As you see, sir, a rail track is constructed, reaching as far as the dip of the coal will allow, when the cars are loaded as you see them just yonder coming out of the mine. Generally, the rocks above the drift are sufficiently compact to bear the weight overhead; but when they are broken and loose, we have to form a roofing of heavy planks, as you see in the mouth of this drift. Nearly all the mines around here are 'water levels,' and are more accessible and free from dangers than any mines in the anthracite regions.

"But here is our train," he added as a small coal-car approached drawn by a mule. (Fig. 17.) In this

FIG. 17.—*Mule Car.*

some temporary seats were arranged, which the party occupied, and soon after were passing the dark opening, the old guide going ahead, where his lamp shed its feeble glare on the gloomy surroundings. It was with an involuntary shudder that the girls saw the fast-receding daylight vanishing in the rear. It grew fainter and fainter until it was but a mere point, like a distant star, and then was lost altogether. Ella clung spasmodically to her father's arm, while Minnie tried to keep her courage up, but with rather a poor show. Milton was so deeply interested that he hardly knew whether he was afraid or not. After passing for quite a distance, seemingly much longer to the young folks than it really was, they began to hear the dull echo of the miners' picks and hammers, and occasionally what seemed to be the sound of strange human voices, giving the whole scene a weird and ghostly aspect that might well try the nerves of one a stranger to such scenes. By and by they caught the glimpse of other lights far ahead, and could hear the rattle of coal as the miners were filling the cars at the end of the gangway. Reaching this point, they saw a number of men busily employed, drilling, breaking, and shoveling coal out of the breasts and filling cars to remove it to the breaker. It was a strange and busy scene.

"Here," said the guide, "we must leave our mule train and try our climbing ability, if you wish to examine further into our mining operations."

Leaving the cars and passing a short distance from the main gangway, the way being quite steep from the dip of the coal-seam, they entered a part of the mine where there seemed to be a number of stalls cut from the bed of coal, with narrow avenues running between them.

"These," said the guide, "are what we call 'breasts.' Of course it will not do to cut away all the coal, for that would let the whole mountain down on our heads—a thing that does sometimes occur, notwithstanding all our caution; so we cut out these chambers, leaving enough coal remaining to support the roof of the mine. When the coal-bed is found somewhat level, we get along quite easily; but this is not often the case, the dip of the vein sometimes leading us a rough-and-tumble course, being tilted and overlapped; with occasionally a great 'fault,' which we have to search out, above or below the floor of the gangway. This gives us steep places to climb, making our work very trying, for we then have a very hard time getting our coal to the cars. But if you can clamber up this way, you can see the men getting the coal from its native bed."

Following the old miner some distance up one of the slopes, they soon heard the heavy blows of the pitmen as they were getting out the coal and breaking it up into manageable lumps. Entering one of the breasts, the dim light of the workers showed a number of stalwart men busily engaged in quarrying the Black Diamond. (Fig. 18.) It was with the deepest interest that the Deans watched the various operations which were going on before them. Some were preparing for blasting; others with picks and

FIG. 18.—*At Work in the Mines.*

crowbars were removing large blocks of coal which had already been loosened by an explosion; while still others with heavy hammers were reducing the lumps to yet smaller dimensions. The men were begrimed and blackened by their employment, with brawny arms and unkempt hair; no wonder, therefore, that the girls shrunk from any near approach to them, though assured by the guide that they were special acquaintances, as this was the place where he was employed at the time.

Pausing here for a more careful inspection of practical mining, Mr. Dean recalled the attention of his children to the grand processes by which God had treasured up the rich deposit of Black Diamonds which they were then examining.

"Every geological fact," said he, "searched out in connection with these coal-mines, indicates that they were formed many thousand feet below the surface of the earth; and whether formed exclusively of the carboniferous vegetation, or in part by the liquefaction of carbonic acid and its subsequent solidification by evaporation—a theory held by some—they are a sublime result of God's goodness and forethought. His infinite benevolence laid the treasure away and locked it up for unknown ages, and then, by an omnipotent grasp, he lifted up the mighty mass of wealth and dropped it on the top of these hills, or thrust its richness out of their sides, to be discovered by the stumbling foot of a poor hunter."

Milton, who had been looking and listening with eyes and ears wide open, now said,

"I once thought that nothing could be less interesting than a piece of dirty coal, but I find how greatly I was mistaken. I never dreamed of such things in connection with it as I have seen to-day. I shall try never to think lightly of anything again."

"Nor should you, my son, for all things are the work of divine hands, and therefore cannot be insignificant. As the angel said to Peter, in the vision on the housetop, respecting the fitness of using certain animals for food, we should call nothing 'common or unclean,' for what the hand of God has touched is sanctified; and all through these mines we can trace the Almighty's handiwork."

"Ah, sir," responded the pious old miner, "you may well say that, and I can testify that the divine Presence pervades these dark places as well, for many of these chambers have I found to be a Bethel, and from one in a mine in the old country I cried unto the Lord when no other arm was able to deliver me, and that 'brought salvation unto me.' You see, sir, I was working in a mine where the vein was rather thin, and the shale above loose and crumbling, so we had to form a roofing of planks, and the floor had a disposition to 'creep'—that is, the pressure from above made it kinder swell up. The fact was, sir, it was a right down dangerous mine, where the lives of the men were risked shamefully to save a few dollars that a 'pack-wall' would have cost. Well, as I was saying, one day as we were working the mine, we put in a big blast, and had it just ready to fire off as the men were preparing to go up the shaft at night, leaving me behind to set off the blast. I fixed the fuse and retired to an old breast a little farther off to wait for the explosion, which soon came, and, unfortunately, not only tore up the coal-bed, but brought a crash all around, the whole roof of the mine being crushed down, filling all the gangways with broken shale. My lamp was extinguished and I had no means of relighting it, and there I was in total darkness. I began to grope my way round to find where I was, and soon, to my horror, found that I was completely shut up in a space of but a few feet in dimensions. My blood seemed to grow thick, my hair stood on end, and I became so weak that I dropped on the damp floor of the breast. After a while I began to feel around, but could find no opening from my dark prison. Neither crack nor crevice seemed to be left, and there I was, sealed up in a deep, dark grave. Weak and faint, I sat down and tried to collect my thoughts. I knew that my wife would soon spread the alarm which my absence would excite, and the men would return to the mine to search after me; but what chance there might be of finding me I knew not, as I did not know the extent of the disaster, and feared just what happened—that they would search for me at the point where the blast was made. I hallooed many times as loud as I could, but heard no response to my cry, nor could I hear any noises indicating that search was being made for me. Oh, how many times I groped around my dark prison and felt every inch of its walls until I knew every dent and projection on them! but no chance of escape was anywhere to be found—I was in a living tomb. After a while I began to grow hungry, and suffered from an intolerable thirst. To satisfy the latter, I found a little spot of muddy sediment in a corner, too thick with coal-dust to drink, but by spreading over it a piece of my coarse shirt I could lick up the small drops which oozed through, which afforded me some relief. At times I sat down and wept like a child as I thought of the terrible agony of my poor wife and children, and of their helpless and dependent condition. Then I fell on my face and cried unto the Lord mightily. I said, 'I am cast out of thy sight, yet I will look again toward thy holy temple;' and he heard the voice of my cry and delivered me. When I arose, I felt quite calm and assured, and for the first time thought of doing what I had not done before—trying the walls with my drill-hammer, which, fortunately, I had with me when the mine caved in. Around my dungeon I went, hitting blow after blow with all the strength I had remaining, and soon struck a place that seemed to sound thin and hollow. Here I repeated my strokes with increased vigor, and to my inexpressible joy a large slab of shale tumbled down, leaving an opening through which I could creep out, which I was not slow in doing. But then I was out of one difficulty only to plunge into another. All was darkness, and I knew not which way to turn, but went creeping here and there, sometimes on my hands and knees, now butting up against some obstruction that barred all farther progress, and then turning to seek an escape in some other direction. Oh, sir, the misery of that horrible journey makes my flesh creep as I think of it. I shouted many times, but no voice came back to give me hope. By and by I thought I heard distant noises, and then cried louder, though I was so weak my voice could hardly have been above a whisper. I felt my strength rapidly failing me, and could no longer stand up, but had to creep along on all fours. While thus putting forth my last efforts for deliverance, my hand touched the rail track, and with the thought that I might now be saved I fainted, and knew no more until I saw the face of my dear wife bending over me as I lay on the grass near the mouth of the shaft. I had been in the pit over three days. In about two hours after the accident the alarm was given, and the men had been seeking me all the time; but, just as I feared, they bent all their efforts to reach the place where the blast was located, which led them farther and farther from the place of my imprisonment. But excuse me, sir; I could not help telling you how God graciously remembered me 'way down in the darkness of that terrible mine; he is, indeed, 'a present help in time of trouble.'"

"You need make no apologies, my dear friend," said Mr. Dean, "for we have all been deeply interested and instructed by your recital. God's hand was very marvelously seen in your deliverance."

"Ay, truly, truly!" was the old man's reply, "but a greater marvel that he should deliver me from going down into the deeper, darker pit of destruction by the precious gift of his only begotten Son, for which I give him greater thanks. But here," he continued, "is a kind of underground office where we receive our visitors, and the young ladies had better rest themselves for a little while."

CHAPTER XV.

MINING THE BLACK DIAMOND.

WHILE the party were resting in the mine, Mr. Dean asked the old guide to give them a general description of the manner of working the mines.

"With great pleasure, sir," was the cheerful reply, "though it's only such information as a plain, unlettered man can give. I don't know much about the big names they give to some of these things, but I know well how to use the pick and the drill, to shape the 'drift' and the 'breast,' or to go up and down the shaft."

"And these are the very things which we wish to learn," said Mr. Dean.

"To be sure, sir; you know all about the hard names and the science of these things better than I do.

"Well, you see, sir, we have two kinds of workings in these regions, since we deserted the open quarry near Summit Hill; one is the 'drift mine,' like this in which we now are—this, as I have already told you, is the usual manner of reaching the coal when it crops out above the water-level of the neighborhood and the dip is not too steep;—the other is called a 'shaft mine,' where we have to seek the coal in deep beds below the surface of the earth, often at the depth of several hundred feet, with the water dripping in all around us."

"That is the character of the mine at Avondale, is it not," asked Mr. Dean, "where the terrible accident occurred in eighteen hundred and sixty-nine?"

"Yes, sir, and you may well say terrible accident, and one that I shall never forget. As soon as I heard of the calamity I went over to the scene of the disaster to lend what aid I could; I couldn't help going. I remembered the agony of those three horrible days when I was buried in the deep, dark mine, but here were scores of my fellow-workmen suffering in the same awful condition. It was at first reported that more than two hundred were in the mine when it took fire, though it turned out that it was not quite so bad, as only one hundred and eight bodies were ever found. But oh, sir, just think of that number of men suffering all the horrors which I endured, and more too! for they had the dreadful fire blazing in the shaft, cutting off all hope of escape, and at the same time driving the fatal gas into all the gangways and workings of the mine.

When I reached the place, there were scores of wives and children gathered round the smouldering breaker, with disheveled hair, wringing their hands, sobbing, and weeping in their despair. There, too, were large groups of strong, brave miners, men who had risked death in many forms, who now stood pale and mute with horror. Oh, sir, it was fearful, it was fearful!"

While the old man was giving vent to his deep emotions at the recollection of the shocking scenes witnessed at Avondale, the girls became blanched with fear and sympathy, and were painfully nervous. The father saw this, and to relieve them said to the old man,

"I do not wonder that you are deeply moved by the sad events which you witnessed, for the whole country was shocked by them; but I fear your recital of them will not be exactly the best preparation for my daughters to enjoy their further rambles in the mines."

"True, true," responded the guide—"I should have thought of that; please excuse me; but when I think of the dreadful scene, I forget myself. A hundred and eight men suffering what I did, and not one of them saved—and I was! Oh, the mercy of God!" This was said in a kind of soliloquy, as though it was hard to banish the horror from his mind or thoughts, when, recollecting himself, he said again, "Excuse me. I was telling you about a shaft mine; but as you are going to Avondale and Scranton and other places, you will go down into some of these deep pits and see just how it is done, so I need not tell you any more about it.

"It is sometimes very hard," continued the guide, "to get at the coal, and we have to dig, drill, and blast, shovel and cart away almost mountains of dirt and stone. Then we have to build walls of stone and logs, and make roofing over the gangways, to protect our heads from falling slate and rocks. Tracks for our mining cars must be laid, some of which we have to push up steep planes and slide down others. Doors to shut out the noxious gases have to be constructed, and various means for ventilation, and a hundred other things attended to, before we make our work safe and profitable. So you see, sir, that a miner has no easy time of it. Besides this, you know that we have to work in the darkness, amid dampness and dirt, with no cheerful sunshine to relieve our labors, so you need not wonder that miners seldom sing or whistle at their work, and hold but little conversation with each other when in the mines. They know that their work is hard and dangerous, and are generally silent and thoughtful.

"In bituminous mines we can generally work out

the coal with our picks and crowbars, but here among the anthracite we have to drill and blast a great deal, which makes our work more dangerous. But these are the main dependence of the miner," said the old man, at the same time showing a pair of picks, one sharp at both ends, while the other had a head used for driving wedges or breaking coal. "Besides these, we have an iron crowbar, a heavy hammer, a shovel and some wedges. The miner generally takes good care of his tools, keeping them sharp and always at hand. Every man working in the mines of course must have his light. When there is no fear of the 'fire-damp,' a little lamp such as I now have on my hat is generally used. Sometimes, when working at a blast or in a breast, we hang our lamps where they will give us the best light, but always carry them with us when we move about. If the 'fire-damp' is known to exist in the mine, we have to use every precaution to avoid explosions, and then carry a 'safety-lamp,' which is constructed wholly or in part of fine wire gauze, through which the flames will not pass so as to ignite the gas. (Fig. 19.) With this light I have often gone into places where the gas was so dense as to make a constant crackling noise, making my very flesh creep, as I did not know how soon I might be blown into eternity. In such cases the careless opening of a lamp or an unfortunate stumble has sent many a poor miner to his final account.

"In old times we used to have many things to do by hand that are now taken off by machinery, especially in getting the coal out of the mines."

"Then there has been some improvement," said

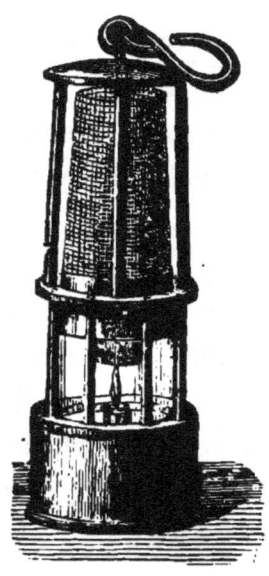

FIG. 19.—*Safety Lamp.*

Mr. Dean, "in the miner's condition—at least, in the tax upon his muscle?"

"Oh, very great, very great," was the reply. "The work used nearly all to be done by hand, and much of it was most inhumanly exacted from young children of both sexes, and it was no uncommon thing to see frail women bearing burdens that would crush one of our modern females."

"Why, you don't mean to say," interrupted Ella, "that women and children were ever employed in such dreadful work as this?"

"Yes, indeed," was the reply. "I went into the mines myself when but a young lad as a 'putter-boy,' and have pushed many a car-load of coal to the shaft, crawling on my hands and knees, and was often assisted by little girls younger than I was. (Fig. 20.) In Scotland women were formerly em-

Fig. 20.—*Children at Work in the Mines.*

ployed to carry baskets of coal up a succession of steep ladders three or four hundred feet. To climb up such long steep ladders is of itself a most trying effort without the addition of a heavy load of coal."

"Wasn't it perfectly barbarous?" said Minnie, indignantly; "and I think we women ought to be devoutly thankful that we are saved from such terrible employment."

"I think your sex, my daughter, owes something to the enlightened spirit of the age, which has put the stamp of barbarity on the employment of women and children at any such inhuman labor. In this respect, one of 'woman's rights' has been very justly recognized in all lands except Belgium, where women are still found with their husbands and brothers, engaged in the severe labors of the pit, some of them often possessing marks of beauty and refinement.

"But we did not come here," continued Mr. Dean, "to discuss questions of political economy, and so we will let these things pass, and listen to what our good friend has to say further about getting out the Black Diamond."

"Well, sir," replied the old man, "if you are all rested and ready for a little more climbing, we will pass through some other parts of the mine, where you can see the men at work, and that will give you a better idea than any words of mine."

Following the guide, they first came to a gang of men employed in "undermining" a bench of coal. This is done, when the coal is of great thickness, by blasting out the bottom of the stratum and carefully picking away its supports, until the mass is easily broken off by a few well-directed blows at the top, assisted by the weight of its own leverage. Pausing before such an operation, they saw men engaged in drilling for blasting, while one was lying at full length on his side, using his pick to remove some obstructions at the base of the mass.

"I should think that must be very hard work," said Mr. Dean.

"You may well say that," was the old man's reply, "and we used to have enough of it to do in the old way of working; but it is only resorted to now when a few strokes of the pick will remove some slight obstruction in the process of undermining, and thereby save a resort to drilling. We sometimes loosen great masses of coal of seventy-five or a hundred tons in this way, and then have to break it up into such pieces as we can load into the cars, in which it is taken to the breaker, where it is reduced to the various sizes found in market.

"One of the most important things in a mine," continued the guide, "is proper ventilation. In all pits, and more especially where they are deep shaft mines, there is a constant and rapid accumulation of foul and explosive gases, which must be got rid of, and we have to drive them out and get fresh air in. The best way to do this is to have two or more shafts; but sometimes this cannot be well accomplished, as where the mine runs in at the base of a high mountain. In such cases we build a great furnace in the mine, and create a draft by heat, or force air through the gangways by machinery. With all our efforts, however, we have to breathe a dangerous and unwholesome atmosphere, uncertain whether the next breath will bring death or life, especially when we get into the remote workings of the mine, often a mile or two from the shaft."

"Your labors are truly severe and hazardous," said Mr. Dean, "and we who enjoy the results so pleasantly around our firesides ought to be grateful to the brave men who provide us with the great requisite of warmth and cheerfulness. But I think it is about time for us to be finding our way out to the daylight again, as the afternoon is well passed and I begin to fear the dampness and chill which I feel creeping over me; and my daughters also, I perceive, are drawing their waterproofs closer about them."

"Perhaps it will be prudent," said the old man, "for the young ladies to get into the sunshine, for this is a damp and gloomy place, in which few would tarry long except upon compulsion. If you will excuse me for a short time, I will have a seat prepared for them if they are not afraid to ride on the top of a load of coal."

"Thank you," was Mr. Dean's reply; "we shall

not be fastidious about the style of our carriage on this occasion."

While waiting for the car to start, the party took a general survey of the surroundings. It was a subterranean labyrinth of gangways, stalls, and working places, with dim flickering lights as the miners moved here and there. Once or twice they were startled and stunned as the loud booming of an exploded blast shook and reverberated through the mine. The constant click of drilling hammers and the duller thud of breaking up coal, the rumble of mine-cars and rattle of coal in filling them, combined with the voices of the mule-drivers and the occasional braying of the animals as they saw some subterranean mate approaching—all made up such a strange medley as to possess quite a fascination notwithstanding the gloomy accessories. But, curiosity once satisfied, the party were quite ready to pass to scenes of a more cheerful character. When, therefore, the old guide announced that he was ready for a start, there was no "longing, lingering look," but a prompt mounting on the load of lump-coal, and a start made for the open air. When they once more caught the distant star-like appearance of the light at the entrance, the girls were delighted, and watched its gradual enlargement with the greatest interest. When, at last, they swept through the entrance of the mine, and came into the broad sunlight, Milton shouted,

"Hurrah for old Sol! We're having two mornings in one day; and I much prefer the old-fashioned one, when the sunlight comes into my window, rather than this afternoon dawning, when one comes out of the mine to seek it."

"Ah, my lad," said the old miner, "if you had spent as many days in the dark mine as I have, you would have learned to appreciate these 'afternoon mornings,' as you call them. It is not often that we enjoy more than two or three hours of sunlight a day, except on the Lord's Day, and that mostly after we come out of the mines when our day's work is done.

"But here we are at the breaker," said the guide; "and if you will keep your seats, we will take you up to the top and let you see how these big lumps of coal are broken into a proper size." (Fig. 21.)

Remaining in the car, they were drawn up into the breaker by the upper track, where the coal is "dumped" into the receiving-chutes and thence descends into the crushing-rolls. Being here broken into irregular sizes, it passes into the screens, which are so formed as to assort the coals, dropping them into the appropriate bins.

All coal is more or less intermixed with slate and

what the miners call "bone," which must be separated by hand. This gives employment to a large number of boys. They seat themselves along the screens as the coal comes from the crushing-rollers, and pick

Fig. 21.—*Coal-Breaker.*

out the refuse as it comes within their reach. On the faithfulness and care of these embryo miners is dependent the quality of our coal. When Mr. Dean and his children passed into that part of the breaker, they saw a large number of these lads at their work. Half clad, blackened, and mischievous, they might easily have been mistaken for a number of ebony imps as they chattered and frolicked at their work. It was not until some of the facetious remarks called attention to the fact, that the girls became aware that their faces were not quite so fair as when they entered the mine.

"I say, Jake," whispered one, at the same time making a gesture toward Minnie, "that gal's got a strata of coal croppin' out 'n her chin, hasn't she?"

"That's so," was the reply; "but just twig that young starchy; his mouth's open wide enough to swallow a whole hunk of coal. I've a notion to pitch a piece of slate into it."

"You'd better be quiet," said another urchin; "old Ben has them in tow, and you know he'd be huffy and report us if you'd offend his company."

Milton and his sisters could not fail to perceive that they were the subjects of remark by the boys, but they entered into the humor of the occasion, which pleased the busy urchins, and they were soon on good terms and had struck up quite a trade with their visitors, offering choice pieces of slate, specimens of minerals, or various little carvings of lumps of coal, some of them being really neatly done.

The old guide explained the various operations of

crushing, cleaning, and sorting coal, and then showed them the chutes down which it was sent in loading the cars. These chutes were constructed immediately under the one by which they had passed into the upper story of the breaker. By running the train of cars under these fixtures, it is loaded in a very few minutes, with no handling of the coal.

After these works had been sufficiently examined, Mr. Dean thanked the faithful and pleasant old man who had escorted them during their visitation, and properly rewarded him, though he was very reluctant to take anything from a minister; and then, as the last train for the day on the Switchback came along, they bade him good-bye and started on their return to Mauch Chunk, well satisfied with their day's excursion.

P

CHAPTER XVI.

THE OLD MINER'S STORY.

"WELL," said Milton, while returning to Mauch Chunk that evening, "I think miners are about the hardest-looking set of men I ever saw. Living down in the darkness and dirt so much, I suppose they naturally become coarse and unfeeling, until they are not more than half human."

"Ah, but, brother," answered Minnie, "that isn't true of the nice old man who was our guide to-day; for though he was roughly clothed and all blackened with coal, he was a real gentleman, and has a kind, loving heart, I know."

"You are right, my daughter," replied the father, "and you might add to his endowments the richer graces of a devout and earnest Christian, for I have seldom met with one who seemed so deeply imbued with the spirit of his divine Master. The remark of your brother may be more or less true, for we cannot altogether resist the influences of our surroundings.

> 'Above the precept deftly urged,
> We take the hue and moulding
> Of scenes that daily meet our gaze,
> Though forced on our beholding.'

"Miners have but little opportunity to converse with each other, because of the noise and din created by their work, as we have had full proof to-day in our visitation, added to which their employment demands the most constant and close attention. They spend but a small portion of the twenty-four hours of a day in the outer world, and that they very naturally devote to walking in the sunshine and social conversation with one another; hence they have but little chance for mental improvement and the cultivation of the graces of refinement. They generally go into the mines in their childhood, and enjoy but few opportunities for mental improvement; yet with all of these disadvantages, the mines have not been without representative men who have been distinguished ornaments in the highest departments of life. As I have already intimated, miners have dropped the pick and the shovel, and passed into Congress as statesmen; they have been distinguished at the Bar and in the pulpit; they have stood high among the men of science and won bright laurels on the field of battle. Among my ministerial acquaintances I number several who began life in the mines of England,

Wales, and in America, and who are now eminent for their learning and eloquence. But among those who remain in the active ranks of the army of miners there are men of the noblest natures, and not a disaster occurs in the coal regions but develops a courage and manhood of the highest character. We glorify men who rush into the forefront of the battle, breasting the leaden storm, but this is no more daring than the act of courage which carries the miner into the burning pit, or the dreaded gallery filled with poisonous or explosive gases, that he may rescue his unfortunate companions. Many noble lives have been thus devoted to the cause of humanity, and let us not say that the ranks which furnished them are wanting in the noblest attributes of manhood because their hands are hardened with toil and their faces begrimed from their employment. The miner not only shows that he has the fullest endowment of manly courage, but that in his social life he is also the subject of the finer sentiments that give a zest and charm to life.

"A number of years ago I met with an interesting story of an old English miner which most beautifully illustrates both the stern manhood and the finer sensibilities of the class. I was so impressed with its simple pathos that I have carefully treasured it up; and to-night, after supper, if you will remind me of it, I will give you the details, and I am sure you will be much interested."

"Thank you, father," said Ella; "I'll see that your memory is kept fresh, for I shall be anxious to hear the story."

"You may be sure of that," responded Milton, "if it is a love story; and perhaps El has some notion of going into the mining business with some of the young pitmen she saw to-day."

"Thank you, brother," replied the sister; "I much prefer to get my coals in another market; but I am anxious to learn everything good respecting the poor men who have to work so hard and face so many dangers to supply us with one of the necessaries of life."

"A very commendable desire, my daughter; and it would be much better for all if we spent more time in trying to learn the good qualities of our neighbors and less in seeking out their vices and faults. But here we are at the foot of Mount Pisgah, and must now bid good-bye to the Switchback."

"Which we do, father," said Milton, "by most heartily thanking you for the privilege we have enjoyed of having a double ride over it."

"Yes," said Minnie, "and so I give papa double thanks for my rides, and will pay compound interest on the debt when I get home."

"Our pleasure has indeed been great," Ella said, "and I am grateful to dear father for it; but somehow I cannot get rid of the idea that we are overtaxing his generosity, and think we ought to be satisfied and return home without making further demands upon it."

"My dear daughter," was the father's response, "I am gratified by your affectionate consideration, but beg that you will not allow any such thoughts to mar the pleasure of our excursion. We can invest what little I have to spare in no better way than to change *cents* into *sense*. Wisdom is better than gold, and your love is a richer dividend than banks can return; so as we are both making a rich investment, let us not be miserly in the transaction."

"Excuse me, father," was Ella's reply; "if love can compensate you, you certainly will be a large gainer by your kind outlay, and so I will not refer to the subject again."

When once more in their cosy room at the hotel, the whole party had a high appreciation of the virtues of soap and water and a keen relish for the supper which soon after followed. When the evening hour brought its coolness and the usual thronging to the verandah of the Mansion House to enjoy the grand scenery and strange medley of the place,

Mr. Dean was reminded by his children of the promised story of the old miner.

"Yes," said Mr. Dean, "you shall have the narrative, and in the old man's language, though I do not know to whom belongs the credit of first giving the interesting recital to the world. Our day's experience will put us into sympathy with the story.

"Well," said the old miner, "it was twenty-five years ago, and I was just twenty-five years old then—working as a regular pitman on the day or night shift. Dirty work, of course, but there was soap in the land, even in those days; and when I came up after a good wash and a change, I could always enjoy a read such times as I didn't go to the night-school, where, always having been a sort of reading fellow, I used to help teach the boys, and on Sundays I used to go to the school and help there.

"Of course it was all done in a rough way, for hands that had been busy with a coal-pick all day were not, you will say, much fit for using the pen at night. However, I used to go, and it was there I found out that teaching was a thing that paid you back a hundred per cent. interest, for you could not teach others without teaching yourself. But—I may as well own it—it was the teaching of the Sunday-school I used to look forward to, mostly, I fear, because it was there I used to see Mary Andrews, the daughter of one of our head-pitmen. He was not very high up, only at the pit-village he lived in one of the best houses and had almost double the wages of an ordinary man. Consequently, Mary Andrews was a little better dressed and better educated than the general run of girls about there, and there was something about her face that used, in its quiet earnestness, to set me anxiously watching her all the time she was teaching, till I used to wake up of a sudden to the fact that the boys in my class were all at play, when, flushing red all over my face, I used to leave off staring over to the girls' part of the big school-room and try to make up for lost time.

"I can't tell you when it began, but at the time I used somehow to associate Mary Andrews' pale, innocent face with everything I did. Every blow I struck into a coal-seam with my sharp pick used to be industry for Mary's sake. Of an evening, when I washed off the black and tidied up my hair, it used to be so that she would not be ashamed of me if we met, which we were pretty sure to do, for somehow my steps always turned toward where she lived. Every time I made my head ache with some calculation out of my arithmetic—ten times as difficult because I had no one to help me—I used to strive and try on till I conquered, because it was all for Mary's sake. Not that I dared to have told her so, I thought, but somehow the influence of Mary used to lift me up more and more, till I no more should have thought of going to join the other pitmen in a public-house than of trying to fly.

"It was about this time that I got talking to a young fellow about my own age who worked in my shift. John Kelsey his name was, and I used to think it a pity that a fine fellow like he was, handsome, stout, and strong, should be so fond of low habits, dog-fighting and wrestling, so popular amongst our men, who enjoyed nothing better than getting over to Sheffield or Rotherham for what they called a day's sport, which generally meant unfitness for work during the rest of the week."

"'Well,' said John, 'your ways seem to pay you;' and he laughed and went away, and I thought no more of it till about a month after, when I found that I was what people who use plain, simple language call in love, and I'll tell you how I found it out. I was going along one evening past old Andrews' house, when the door opened for a moment as though some one was coming out; but as if I had been seen, it was closed directly. In that short moment, though, I had heard a laugh, and that laugh I was sure was John Kelsey's. I felt on fire for a few moments as I stood there, unable to move, and then, as I dragged myself away, the feeling that came over me was one of blank misery and despair. I could have leaned my head up against the first wall I came to and cried like a child, but that feeling passed off, to be succeeded by one of rage; for as the blindness dropped from my eyes, I saw clearly that not only did I dearly love Mary Andrews—love her with all a strong man's first love, such a love as one could feel who had till now made a sole companion of his books—but that I was forestalled, that John Kelsey was evidently a regular visitor there, and, for aught I knew to the contrary, was her acknowledged lover. I did not like playing the spy; but with a faint feeling of hope on me that I might be mistaken, I walked back past the house, and there was no mistake: John Kelsey's head was plain enough to be seen on the blind, and I went home in despair.

"How I looked forward to the next Sunday! half resolved to tell Mary of my love and to ask her if there was any truth in that which I imagined, though I almost felt as if I should not dare.

"Sunday came at last, and somehow I was rather late when I entered the great school-room, one end of which was devoted to the girls and the other to the boys. At the first glance I saw that Mary was in her place; at the second, all the blood in my body seemed to rush to my heart, for there, standing talking to the superintendent, was John Kelsey, and the next minute he had a class of the youngest children given to him, and he was hearing them read. He has done this on account of what I said to him was my first thought, and I was glad; but directly after I was in misery, for my eyes rested on Mary Andrews, and that explained it all—it was for her sake he had come.

"I don't know how that afternoon passed, nor anything else, only that as soon as the children were dismissed I saw John Kelsey go up to Mary's side and walk home with her; and then I walked out up the hillside, wandering here and there among the mouths of the old, unused pits half full of water, and thinking to myself that I might just as well be down in one of them, for there was no more hope or pleasure for me in this world.

"Time slipped on, and I could plainly see one thing that troubled me sorely: John was making an outward show of being a hard-working fellow, striving hard for improvement, so as to stand well in old Andrews' eyes, while I knew for a fact that he was as drunken and dissipated as any young fellow that worked in the pit. I could not tell Andrew this, nor I could not tell Mary. If she loved him, it would grieve her terribly, and be dishonorable as well, and perhaps he might improve. I can tell him, though,

I thought, and I made up my mind that I would; and meeting him one night evidently hot and excited with liquor, I spoke to him about it.

"'If you truly love that girl, John,' I said, 'you will give up this sort of thing.' He called me a meddling fool, and said he had watched me, that he knew that I had a hankering after her myself, but she only laughed at me, and one way and another so galled me that we fought. I went home that night bruised, sore, and ashamed of my passion, while he went to Andrews and said he had been compelled to thrash me for speaking insultingly about Mary. I heard this afterward, and don't know how it was, but I wrote to tell her it was false, and that I loved her too well ever to have acted so. When we next met, I felt that she must have read my letter and laughed at me. At all events, John Kelsey did, and I had the mortification of seeing that old Andrews evidently favored his visits.

"John still kept up his attendance at the school, but he was at the far end; and more than once when I looked up it was to find Mary Andrews with her eyes fixed on me. She lowered them though, directly, and soon after it seemed to me that she turned them on John. I thought it was quite wrong to let my thoughts be so distracted on the holy day, and tried to forget all about Mary and John, but it was very hard, I tell you, and thus I struggled on until near Christmas.

"One evening when I was to go on the night shift, I sat dreamy and listless over my supper, when all at once I heard the startling cry,

"'The pit's fired! the pit's fired!' and there was not a soul that did not know it, for the pit had spoken for itself in a voice of thunder that shook the whole village. As I hurried out I thought, all in a flash like, of what a day it would be for some families there; but my dreaming soon became a reality as I saw the poor distracted women shrieking and running here and there calling for their husbands and sons. I didn't lose no time, as you may suppose, in running to the pit's mouth, but those who lived nearer were there long before me; and by the time I got there I found that the cage had brought up part of the men and those who were insensible, and that it was just going down again. It went down directly; and just as it disappeared, who should come running up, pale and scared, but Mary Andrews? She ran right up to the knot of men who had come up, and who were talking loudly, in a wild, frightened way, about how the pit had fired—they could not tell how —and she looked from one to the other and then at the men who were scorched, and then she ran to the pit's mouth, where I was.

"'There is no one belonging to you down there?' I asked her.

"'Oh yes, yes! my father was down, and John Kelsey.'

"As she said the first words I was ready for anything; but when she finished the sentence, a cold chill came over me, and she saw the change, and looked at me in a strange, half-angry way. 'Here comes the cage up,' I said, trying hard to recover myself, and going up to the bank by her side; but when a half dozen scorched men stepped out and we looked at their disfigured faces, poor Mary gave a low wail of misery, and I heard her say, softly,

"'Oh, father! father! father!'

"It went right to my heart to hear her bitter cry, and I caught hold of her hand. 'Don't be downhearted, Mary,' I said, huskily; 'there's hope yet.' Her eyes flashed through her tears as she turned sharply on me; and pressing her hand for a moment, I said, softly, 'Try and think more kindly of me, Mary.' And then I turned to the men. 'Now, then, who's going down?' I shouted.

"'You can't go down,' shouted half a dozen voices; 'the choke got 'most the better of us.'

"'But there are two men down!' I cried, savagely. 'You are not all cowards, are you?' Two men stepped forward, and we got into the cage.

'Who knows where Andrews was?' I cried; and a faint voice from one of the injured men told me. Then I gave the warning, and we were lowered down, it having been understood that at the first signal we made we were to be drawn up sharply. The excitement kept me from being frightened, but there was a horrid feeling of oppression in the air as we got lower and lower, and twice over the men with me were for being drawn up.

"'It steals over you before you know it,' said one.

"'It laid me like in a sleep when Rotherby pit fired,' said the other.

"'Would you leave Andrews to die?' I said, and they gave in.

"We reached the bottom, and I found no difficulty in breathing and shouting to the men to come on. I ran in the direction where I had been told I should find Andrews, but it was terrible work, for I expected each moment to encounter the deadly gas that had robbed so many men of their lives. But I kept on, shouting to those behind me, till all at once I tripped and fell over some one, and as soon as I could get myself together I lowered the lamp I carried, and to my great delight I found it was Andrews. Whether dead or alive, I could not tell then, but we lifted him amongst us, and none too soon, for as I took my first step back I reeled, from a curious, giddy feeling which came over me. 'Run, if you can,' I said, faintly, for my legs seemed to be sinking under me. I managed to keep on, though, and at our next turn we were in pure air; but we knew it was a race for life, for the heavy gas was rolling after us, ready to quench out our lives if we slackened our speed for a minute. We finally reached the cage, rolled into it more than climbed, and were drawn up, to be received with bursts of cheers, Mary throwing her arms around her father's neck, and sobbing hysterically.

"'I am not much hurt,' he said, feebly, the fresh air reviving him, and he was laid gently down.

"'God bless those brave men who brought me up,' he said; 'but there's another man down—John Kelsey.'

"No one spoke, no one moved, for all knew of the peril we had just escaped from.

"'I can't go myself,' continued Andrews, 'or I would; but you mustn't let him lie there and burn. I left him close up to the lead. He tried to follow me, but the falling coal struck him down. I believe the pit's on fire.'

"There was a loud murmur amongst the men, and some of the women wailed aloud, but still no one moved except old Andrews, who struggled up on one arm, and looked at us, his face black and his whiskers and hair all burnt off.

"'My lads,' he said, feebly, 'can't you do nothing to save your mate?'

"And as he looked wildly from one to the other, I felt my heart like in my mouth.

"'Do you all hear?' said a loud voice, and I started as I saw Mary Andrews rise from where she had knelt holding her father's hand.

"'Do you all hear?' she repeated; 'John Kelsey is left in the pit. Are you not men enough to go?'

"'Men can't go,' said one of the day shift, gruffly; 'no one could live there.'

"You have not tried,' again she said, passionately. 'Richard Oldshaw,' she said, turning to me, with a red glow upon her face, 'John Kelsey is down there dying and asking for help. Will you not go and try to save him?'

"'And you wish me to go, then?' I said, bitterly.

"'Yes,' she said. 'Would you have your fellow-creature lie there and die when God has given you the power and the strength and knowledge to save him?'

"We stood there then, gazing into one another's

eyes. 'You love him so that you can't even help risking my life to save his, Mary. You know how dearly I love you, and that I am ready to die for your sake; but it seems hard, very hard, to be sent like this.' Then I took her hand and kissed it, when she gave mine a gentle pressure and turned her blushing face away. This fired my soul, and I stepped to the pit's mouth, where the men stood in blank silence, and said, 'I'll go down,' and there was a regular cheer rose up as I said these words; but I hardly heeded it, for I was looking at Mary, and my heart sank within me as I saw her standing there smiling with joy. 'Ah,' thought I, 'that pressure was just given to induce me to save John; but I'll do it if I die in the attempt, and may God forgive her, for she has broken my heart.' The next minute I stepped into the cage alone, and it began to move, when a voice called out:

"'This will never do, to let Dick Oldshaw go alone with dozens of strong men looking on. I'll go with him!'

"And a brave young pitman stepped to my side— just the man of the whole crowd whom I would have chosen. Just as we were descending through the opening, I saw Mary Andrews falling back senseless in the arms of the women. Then all was dark, and I was nerving myself for what I had to do. To go by the way in which we had found Andrews I knew was impossible; but I had hopes that by going round by one of the old workings we might reach him, and I told my companion what I thought.

"'That's right—of course it is,' he said, slapping me on the back; 'that comes of books, it does. I wish I could read and know something like you, Dick.'

"Turning short off as soon as we reached the bottom, I led the way, holding my lamp high and climbing and stumbling over the slate that had fallen from the roof; for this part of the mine had not been worked for years. Now we were in parts where we could breathe freely, and then working along where the dense gas made our lamps sputter and crackle; and the opening of one for an instant would have been a flash, and death for us both. Passing on, we were gradually nearing the point where the accident occurred, and became aware of the air setting in a strong draught in the direction in which we were going, and, soon after, we could make out a dull glow, and then there was a deep roar. The pit was indeed on fire, and blazing furiously, so that as we got nearer, trembling—I'm not ashamed to own it, for it was an awful sight—there was the coal growing of a fierce red heat; but, fortunately, the draught set toward an old shaft fully a quarter of a mile farther on, and so we were able to approach, till, with a cry of horror, I leapt over heap after heap, torn from roof and wall by the explosion, to where, close by the fire, lay the body of John Kelsey—so close that his clothes were already smouldering and the fire scorched my face as I laid hold of him and dragged him away. How we got him to the foot of the shaft I cannot tell. I have only a dim recollection of staggering through the mine with our burden, and falling into the cage, and of hearing cheer after cheer, as the dim light broke upon me, and then all was blank for more than a month. I first became conscious that a tender arm was under my head and a tearful warm cheek pressed to mine; and when I opened my eyes, they met those of Mary Andrews. She had been my constant nurse during all those hours when I lingered between life and death, and had brought back the fitful pulse to its life-beat by her tender care. When sufficiently restored, she told me that the explosion had been caused by John Kelsey carelessly lighting his pipe in the mine, that his visits to her had been by her father's wish, but that her heart had always been mine, and that now her hand was ready to go with it whenever I saw fit to accept it, which, you may judge, I was not very slow in doing. And so you have my story, and have already guessed that Mary Andrews that was is now my dear wife.

"In the light of this narrative, my son," said Mr. Dean, "what do you think of the miner's claim to manhood and refinement of character?"

"Why, father, the old man you have told us about had every element of nobility, and I was no doubt wrong in forming my opinion of the class because of the roughness of their appearance when at work. I will try and not form so hasty an opinion again."

"Very good, my son; that is just the lesson I wished to impress upon you when I gave you the story. Fine clothes and a polished address are not always indicative of refinement of character, though we are too apt to associate them together. But now I will leave you to enjoy your watching of the busy scenes before you, while I go and give your mother a description of our wanderings; only do not be too late in your hours, as we shall start on our journey into the beautiful valley of the Wyoming in the morning; so good-night, and pleasant dreams."

CHAPTER XVII.

VISIT TO A SHAFT MINE.

"GOOD-MORNING," said Mr. Dean, pleasantly, as he greeted his young folks in the sitting-room; "I hope you have enjoyed a good night's rest."

"Why, papa," replied Minnie, "I couldn't more than half sleep last night, for I was all the time wandering through dark mines or starting at terrific explosions. I guess your story of the old miner must have made me a little nervous."

"Ah, Min," said Milton, "it was from eating such a big supper of trout last night, rather than from an excess of sympathy."

"That may be, brother, but I don't think the landlord made much on your board-bill last night, either."

"No, that's so, and I don't mean he shall this morning," replied the brother, "for I feel sharp set for my breakfast, I tell you."

"I am very glad that your trip is giving you so good a digestion," said the father, "only be careful not to so indulge the appetite as to destroy the healthy influence. But now let us be preparing for our trip up the Lehigh, for which we have a delightful day."

After a hearty breakfast, the party were escorted to the cars by the ever-cheerful porter.

"Good-bye, Massa Dean," was his parting salute; "hopes you had a good time and will soon make us anodder call at de Mansion House. All 'board, gem'men; train's startin' for Wilkesbarre and Scranton."

Then came the engineer's signal, and the train was off, Mr. Dean's stopping-place being Pittston, where he had a special acquaintance, extensively engaged in mining operations, who had invited him to make a visit to the vicinity, with a promise of his assistance in whatever explorations he might feel disposed to make.

Passing up the Lehigh, the grand and varied scenery kept the young folks in a constant state of wonder and delight. When near White Haven, their attention was especially arrested by an immense "log-jam," and Milton exclaimed,

"What in the world is that, father?" at the same time pointing to the densely-packed mass of logs, extending as far as the eye could see, and in some places heaped in vast piles one upon another.

"That is what is called a 'log-jam,' my son. It is composed of saw-logs which have been cut on the head-waters of the Lehigh and its tributaries and rolled into the water to be carried down by the first flood to the mills and sawed into lumber. The river was so improved a few years ago by locks and dams that logs could be floated down at almost any season; but the great flood of eighteen hundred and sixty-two swept nearly all of them away, and the raftsmen now have to depend on the chance floods of spring or the falling of a heavy rain. We shall see the marks of this disastrous freshet all the way up the river. It was so sweeping in its destruction that no efforts have been made to repair its damages above Mauch Chunk.

"In these log-jams," continued Mr. Dean, "we have, perhaps, a key to the manner in which some of the thicker coal-measures were formed. By some powerful agency—a deluge or an earthquake—large forests of the carboniferous growth were broken off or uprooted, and drifted into some of the deep basins, buried by an avalanche of clay and rocks, and then, by the usual agencies, transformed into coal. If this large collection of logs which we are now beholding were buried hundreds of feet below the surface, shut out from the air, and subjected to enormous pressure and great heat, they would be carbonized like the woods in the coal-pit. Yet in this condition they would preserve enough of their characteristics to enable us to distinguish the different varieties—pine, hemlock, and oak. After examining these logs, we could go to the distant hills and valleys where they grew, and finding stumps and tops, could reconstruct the various trees of which these logs were a part; the reconstruction would be ideal, and yet true to the native models.

"An instance," continued Mr. Dean, "illustrating this fact, occurred in the recent great fire in Boston. Among the other buildings consumed were some large storehouses filled with wheat. After the fire, when the laborers were clearing away the rubbish, large quantities of this grain were found underneath the piles of granite, pressed into large, compact masses, and completely carbonized, bearing a perfect resemblance to the lumps of coal taken from the mines, formed there by the accumulation of the seeds and cones of the carboniferous vegetation. This wheat-coal broke with a vitreous fracture, like mine-coal, and burnt with equal ease, giving off an intense volume of heat. In this striking fact we have, perhaps, a satisfactory solution of the manner in which the enormous primeval forests were transformed into the equally marvelous mountains of coal. Heat and pressure were the mighty potencies which God employed to accomplish this great work of benevolence."

"Yes, I see it all, father," said Milton; "and isn't it wonderful how science can trace out the truth when it has but a single small fact to begin with?"

"Yes, my son; God's works, though expressed in almost an infinite variety of forms, are yet comprehended in one grand unity, where

> 'All are but parts of one stupendous whole,
> Whose body nature is, but God the soul.'

Nor is it possible to detach any one thing, however small and insignificant, from its sublime relations. We may change its external form and give it new combinations, but we cannot sever it from its great companionship. If, therefore, we have but the smallest fact to begin with, and follow that, it will lead us to other correlative facts, until we are arrested by a consciousness of standing in the awful presence of the great Creator of all things. It is only when we turn aside from the leadings of the truth to speculate and theorize—too often, it is feared, from a dread of meeting the divine Architect to whom nature is surely leading—that the mind is confused and the reason baffled. Every aspect of nature reveals a God, but the unrenewed heart, even with its blunted moral sense, invests the divine Being thus made known with attributes so inharmonious with its own nature that there is no desire for fellowship, and hence it prefers to stop short of the final truth. Such men, though they profess to love and seek after wisdom, become 'vain in their imagination,' and 'then their foolish hearts are darkened,' in which condition they are prepared to 'change the truth of God into a lie,' and the natural result is 'vile affections' and a 'reprobate mind' disqualified to study nature or enjoy life."

This conversation was held as the train delayed for a short time near the log-jam; but they were soon again whirling on their way along the sharp turns and winding grades of the railroad, until they swept into the world-renowned Wyoming Valley, celebrated alike for its surpassing beauty and tragic history. These have both been so often described that they need no further repetition:

"But high in amphitheatre above,
    Gay-tinted woods their massy foliage threw;
Breathed but an air of heaven, and all the grove
    As if instinct with living spirit grew,
Rolling its verdant gulf of every hue;
    And now suspended was the pleasing din,
Now from a murmur faint it swelled anew,
    Like the first note of organ heard within
Cathedral aisle ere yet its symphony begin."

Those who have enjoyed a first view of the scenes through which the railroad passes from Mauch Chunk to Wilkesbarre and Pittston will understand the rapt enthusiasm of Milton and his sisters, who, as the car was not crowded, were running from side to side, watching the grand and ever-changing panorama. Every mile of the way brings some enchanting landscape into view, only to be displaced by one perchance more enchanting still.

It is no wonder, therefore, if they were so absorbed that they took no note of time, and were surprised when the conductor called out, "Pittston!" and found they were just in time for dinner.

After dinner, and while the girls were arranging a proper toilet, Mr. Dean sought out his friend, and was soon at the door with a carriage to convey the party to the Eagle shaft, made famous by a terrible disaster in August, eighteen hundred and seventy-one, by which a large number of lives were lost. Arriving at the shaft, they were met by Mr. Dean's friend, who was to be their conductor for the afternoon's excursion under ground. While they were getting ready to descend into the mine, the young folks approached the mouth of the pit, and the first eager look into the deep darkness below made them start back and shudder at the thought of going down into it.

Black Diamonds. Page 253.
Safety Cage.

"Why, father," asked Ella, "we're not going down that deep hole, are we?"

"If we go into the mine, my daughter, I suppose it will have to be in that direction, as there does not appear to be any other way to get there."

"Oh dear!" was the daughter's response; "this is worse than going up Mount Pisgah, for we could see something there."

"There is no occasion to fear, Miss Dean," said their conductor; "we are using the safety-carriages, which are constantly bringing up loads of coal much heavier than our combined weight."

"Thank you, sir," was Ella's reply; "I presume there is no great danger, but the mode of conveyance is rather too perpendicular to suit my notions of safe travel, and the prospect too limited; but I will try and not annoy you with my timidity."

Just then a load of coal came up the shaft, and it was seen at once how perfectly safe the descent would be. This much relieved the anxiety of the sisters, though the spice of danger and adventure just suited the disposition of Milton. The shaft was nearly two hundred feet deep, and was chosen by Mr. Dean from this fact, as he did not wish to overtax the courage of his daughters too much on the first descent, lest he should spoil their enjoyment altogether.

After some hesitation they all stepped into the carriage, and at the proper signal began to descend; and though the mouth of the shaft seemed very large when they stood above it, it now began to contract with a rapidity that was startling—indeed, it almost seemed to fall together over their heads. Down, down they went, until, looking up to the opening, it appeared only like a small single star seen in the zenith on a dark night. The sight made even Milton look sober and anxious. But everything went on gently and smoothly until they reached the "headings," which was the landing-place. Stepping out of the carriage, it was seen at a glance that shaft-mining was quite different from the workings in the "drift" which they had visited at Mauch Chunk. As soon as they were safely landed the gentlemanly conductor began to explain the working of the mine by saying,

"In carrying on operations where the coal lies deep beneath the surface, the first thing is to sink a shaft, which is always carried down through the stratum of coal we wish to work. These shafts vary in size, being from a dozen to twenty feet in diameter; and when the rocks through which we pass are not compact enough to make it safe, it is made so by walling up with bricks or stone. Then we arrange our hoisting machinery, now universally moved by

Black Diamonds.   Page 255.
Old Way of Descending Mines.

steam, though once done by hand or horse-power, and quite often consisting of a single rope containing a loop, into which the miner placed his foot. Then tubs were substituted, giving way, in turn, to platforms, and these were laid by for various patterns of safety-cages and carriages. These last are so constructed as to run on guides, with springs adjusted in such a manner that even should the cable break the carriage would be safe. Many sad accidents occurred in the old ways of descending into the mines, but with our present improvements they are of rare occurrence.

"When our shaft is constructed, we turn our 'headings,' placed directly opposite each other, and driven in some twenty feet, making a capacious landing, such as that in which we are now standing. When this is done, we sink our shaft twenty or thirty feet deeper, forming what miners call a 'sump,' which, in other words, is but a large reservoir, into which we turn all the water that collects in the mine, often in such quantities as to become very troublesome and dangerous. In this we place our steam-pumps, which generally are kept constantly going to keep the water down to a safe level. The shaft is now ready for the carriages, and the working commences. The headings are driven into the mines, but only about ten feet wide, and then air-chambers are constructed parallel to these, a few feet wider, the thickness between them generally being about twenty feet, and entrances made from one to the other at distances of twenty feet or more. But as soon as a new entrance is opened the old one

Fig. 22.—*Plan of Working Mines.*

is closed up, in order to keep the air circulating in the face of the work where the men are directly employed. (Fig. 22.)

"The 'headings' are always driven on a water-level, but the 'breasts,' or chambers, follow the dip, and are turned from the air-ways. These 'breasts' are of various widths, depending very much on the nature of the workings.

"Entrances are cut from one of these to the other, just as in the headings, and for the same purpose— to keep the fresh air in the face of the workings. To support the roof, we leave pillars or use props as often as the nature of the case may require, sometimes working out the former when the mine is about to be abandoned.

"In very extensive mines water often accumulates so rapidly as to become very troublesome and dangerous. When this is the case, we have to enlarge our 'sump,' which is done by driving a dip a short distance from the shaft, working out the coal, and then, by a cut through to the old 'sump,' making quite a subterranean lake, often capacious enough to hold all the water that may accumulate while we are mending our pumps.

"In anthracite mines we depend mainly on blasting out the coal, but in bituminous works the pick and wedges are generally sufficient, with an occasional resort to powder.

"For transporting our coal from the breasts to the shaft, we use mules or light horses, and occasionally have quite an amusing scene in getting them into the mine, as some of them on first going down are perfectly paralyzed with fear. It is only under peculiar circumstances, where mules cannot be used, that men are now employed in pushing the cars.

"Besides premature explosions, falling rocks, caving shafts, and flooding, we have to contend with several more subtle foes in the shape of deadly gases— the 'black-damp,' or carbonic acid gas; the 'white-damp;' the 'after-damp,' or 'choke,' which remains after explosions. All of these will destroy life when present in large volume; but the greatest terror we have to contend with here is carburetted hydrogen gas, or 'fire-damp.' It is much lighter than the atmosphere, and fills all parts of the mine; and being colorless and almost without odor, the doomed miner sometimes walks unconsciously into the deadly magazine, and the next moment is in eternity. Such a terrible event happened to us in August, 1871. Horrors like those I hope never to witness again, and even now shudder when I think of the sad scenes.

"To give you some idea of the curiosities and dangers of mining, we will visit a rock tunnel cut to find a 'fault' which occurred in our mine."

Following their conductor into a distant part of the working, they approached what seemed to be a termination of the mine.

"Here," said he, "we were suddenly arrested in

our operations; and judging from the indications that a fault had occurred, or, as the miners designate it, a 'jump down,' we began boring to determine how deep the displacement was, which turned out to be near forty feet."

"I beg pardon for interrupting you," said Mr. Dean, "but I have been trying to explain to my children some facts in reference to the coal-formations, and among others the nature of a 'fault;' and now, with the facts before them, a little attention will give them a clear idea of the phenomenon. Will you, therefore, be kind enough to show us the peculiarities of the formation?"

"Most willingly," was the prompt reply. "If you will observe the face of this working, you will notice that the coal-seam butts suddenly up against the slate rock, as if it terminated here. From our previous knowledge of the coal-beds, we know that this could not be so, but that a displacement had occurred, and one part either had been pushed up or jumped down, and would be found again by searching in the right direction. In this case we knew that the seam lay below, and the only question was as to the depth at which it could be found. Let us now go down the shaft, and I will show you the other half of the seam, fitting this in all respects, showing conclusively that they were once joined together.

The result is the same as will be witnessed on a small scale if we take a pile of pasteboard, the upper half black and the lower white, then cut it in two pieces, and press down one half until the upper black stratum comes opposite the lower white one."

"Thank you," said Mr. Dean; "your statement is very clear. Do you fully understand the subject now, Milton?"

"Oh yes," was the reply, "and it is very curious and interesting. What a mighty power it must have been to thus rend these mighty rocks asunder, and lift up the very mountains as I would a small pile of paper!"

"You may well say that, my son; but God takes up the mountains as a very little thing. In this way he unlocked the treasures of the earth as easily as we open the door leading to our coal-cellar; and the same benevolent hand that turned the key thousands of years ago is opened to-day to give us our daily bread. But I am deeply interested in the description which I have interrupted, and will not divert further attention from it."

"In our boring to find the lost stratum of coal," resumed the guide, "we soon struck what the miners call a 'blower'—that is, a fissure in the rock—from which poured out a stream of fire-damp in large volume. The workmen had to extinguish their lights and run immediately to save their lives. After waiting a sufficient time they returned, and with their coats and brush from the trees drove out the gas, so that they could resume work. This process had to be repeated several times before we reached the lost coal-seam, as we passed through a succession of blowers. As some of these fissures seemed to be regular gas fountains, we had to provide for its consumption before we could work with safety; so we walled them up with brick and cement, and put two-inch pipes in them perforated with small holes once in twenty inches, and extended them up each side of the tunnel. When these were all lighted, they made a brilliant display; and we thought we had got rid of our gas and obtained a cheap light, but we were soon undeceived, for it was found that our men became exhausted and could not work more than half time; and seeking for the cause, we discovered that as all the air which passed into this inner shaft had to pass through these rows of burners, it was deprived of so much of its oxygen as to be unfit for the purpose of respiration. To remedy this, the perforations in the tubes were closed up and they were extended into the main air-shaft, and the danger was removed, as the volatile gas rushed at once to the surface. Since then we have worked the lower seam with more ease and safety."

"These facts are very interesting," said Mr. Dean, "and we are very much obliged to you, sir, for the information you have given us."

"You are certainly quite welcome," was the reply of the gentlemanly official, "to any information I may be able to communicate, and to explore our mines as extensively as you may desire."

In accordance with this kind offer, the party were conducted through various sections of the mine, visiting the stalls where the mules were kept and other interesting arrangements; but as the manner of getting out the coal was much the same as in the mine already visited, the details need not be repeated.

Having taxed both mind and body about as much as was judicious for one day, Mr. Dean thanked his kind friend and conductor, and then they were soon again mounting the shaft to the daylight above, which was hailed with even more delight than when leaving the drift mine at Summit Hill.

After supper they resorted to the verandah of their hotel, and though the scenery around Pittston is not without attractions, they soon realized the difference from the never-tiring variety and grandeur of Mauch Chunk, and were not reluctant when the hour came to say good-night and seek their pillows, which were very welcome after the exertion of the day.

CHAPTER XVIII.

THE TRAGEDY OF AVONDALE.

"YOU remember," said Mr. Dean, when about to start for Plymouth the next morning, "how much you were interested in the sketch of the disaster at Avondale given us by the old guide at Summit Hill, and noticed how deeply the event had been impressed upon his memory. To-day it is my purpose to take you to the scene of that sad occurrence, and my friend has consented to go with us, through whose agency we shall find ready admittance to the mine and visit the exact location of the tragedy."

"Oh, father," inquired the timid Ella, "will there be no danger in going into the place now? It is fearful to think of such a terrible providence."

"We need dread nothing beyond the ordinary contingencies, my daughter, for the calamity was the result of a fearful crime, although for months regarded as purely accidental."

"I am very anxious to visit the place," said Milton, "ever since I heard the old man's story, for it was of the most thrilling interest, and the events at Avondale were much like those of his adventure, except his personal experience. I don't see why the unsurpassed bravery of the noble-hearted miners should not make the dark battle-scenes where they contend with such fearful adversaries as famous as the deeds of the soldier do the battle-fields above ground."

"So, in truth, they do, my son; for the courage they display is truly unsurpassed, and the object is really more commendable, for the miner faces death only to rescue the lives of others, not to destroy them. But here comes our kind friend to conduct us to the cars."

It being but a short ride from Pittston to Plymouth, the end of the journey was soon reached, and they repaired directly to the mine, which is in the immediate vicinity. At the period of Mr. Dean's visitation, no reminiscences remained to indicate to the traveler the dreadful event that had once turned it into an Aceldama. Proceeding at once to the mine, the presence of the gentlemanly official procured them ready admittance to the workings, attended by one of the men employed in the mine when the disaster occurred—a man of more than usual intelligence among his class. He had been one of the active participants in the efforts to recover the bodies of his doomed companions, and retained a vivid recollection of the scenes of that awful visitation.

The Avondale mine is situated in the Wyoming Valley, on the steepest and most commanding side of the Shawnee Hills. It is one of the best mines in the whole valley, producing near one thousand tons of coal daily. At the time of the calamity there was but one entrance into the mine, and that was situated under the coal-breaker—a very unfortunate arrangement, as events proved. The shaft was sunk to the depth of two hundred and thirty-seven feet, with a capacity of twenty-six feet in length by twelve wide, divided in the centre by a board partition, making two perpendicular avenues, down one of which the carriages and pure air were passed, while the noxious gases were forced up the other.

When the party had landed at the "headings" at the foot of the shaft, their guide said, pointing to galleries which were driven into the mine just in front of them,

"Here are the main entrances into the workings upon which the men were employed at the time of the accident, and to the right the air-way is cut, running directly into the mine, while the gangways curve to the right and left. The right-hand gangway is about twelve hundred feet long, while the left is only two-thirds this length. Following up the airway some two hundred and twenty feet, we come to the fire-furnace used at the time of the conflagration, and from which the fire was supposed to have originated at the time. But some years after the occurrence a poor wretch on his deathbed revealed the dreadful fact that it was set on fire out of sheer revenge." (Fig. 23.)

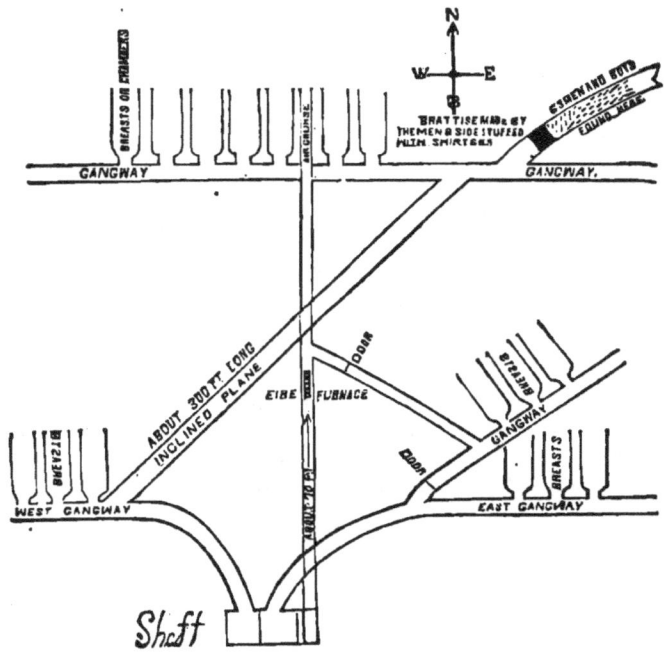

Fig. 23.—*Plan of Avondale Mine.*

"I should think," interrupted Mr. Dean, "that reflection over the awful results of such diabolical wickedness would have shortened the days of any one but a demon incarnate."

"You may well say that, sir," replied the conductor; "for it really did shorten the days of some of the innocent ones who witnessed the calamity and lost dear loved ones by it. I have felt ten years older ever since it occurred.

"On the morning of the sixth of September, eighteen hundred and sixty-nine," he continued, "the shaft down which we have just come was found to be on fire near the bottom, and the flames swept with astonishing rapidity to the top, involving the breaker and surroundings in the general ruin. We tried our best, but we could not check nor control the flames, though we fought them in the agony of desperation, for we knew that more than one hundred of our fellow-workmen were in the mine, cut off from all hope of escape until the fire was subdued. Oh, sir, if you could have seen the crowd of phrensied women, pale as ghosts, who stood there wringing their bloodless hands, begging us to save their husbands and sons, and the greater throngs of children sobbing as though their hearts would break, crying, 'Oh, papa! papa!' you would not have wondered that we strained every muscle and fought the flames with scorched hands and burnt hair and eyebrows. But what could we do with a well of fire more than two hundred feet deep shooting up an immense volume of flames like a huge fountain?

"But, sir, if our agony was so great, just think of what those hundred and eight men must have felt when they rushed to the foot of the shaft, and took the first look up that more than two hundred feet of fire, knowing well that through that seething avenue lay their only possible way of escape! I knew them all, and braver men never lived. Many of them were devout Christians, and could have met death without a tremor in any ordinary way that Providence might appoint; but to see the grim spectre come thus suddenly with its dread message for those scores of strong men, to snatch them away down there in the darkness, with no tender and loving farewell from wife or children, no benediction from stricken parents—that must have been an agony that baffles imagination!

"But confounded as they must have been, they could not stand there long aghast at the hopelessness of reaching the upper world, for they well knew that the burning shaft was sucking up its fiery throat all the fresh air the mine contained, and that very soon a foe equally as fatal would leap upon them from behind—the dreaded black-damp, one full breath of which would stretch them all as blackened corpses. We who work in the mines and know something of its dangers can imagine the whole scene of horrors. To go up through the burning shaft was impossible; to stand there was certain death. There was but one course that presented a ray of hope, and to that they turned. They had a splendid foreman—Hugh Evans. He was brave, self-possessed, and knew his business well, and had faced death in many a mine. We know the course they pursued almost as well as though we had been in the mine and witnessed the whole proceeding; and if you will follow me, we will go over the same ground, and I can point out to you the various attempts they made to escape their doom."

They were led up the gangways; and passing the diagonal to the right, the guide stopped at a certain point, and said,

"Here the poor fellows made their first effort to escape by erecting a barrier of coal-'culm' and stopping the crevices with their clothing, hoping thereby to prevent what pure air there might be in the back of the mine from being drawn up the shaft. But they were soon driven away by the approach of the deadly gas, and retreated a little farther up this diagonal, passing the parallel gangway, where they built a similar barrier, using a mine-car and stuffing it as closely around as possible. The poisonous enemy, however, was close upon them, giving notice of his advent, as one man fell just outside the barricade. Step this way a little farther. Now we are standing on the very spot where the last terrible struggle was made with death. Here sixty-three poor victims were found, men and boys, stripped of their clothing, which they had stuffed into the cracks of the barrier, stark and stiff."

The party stood in that death-chamber with bared heads, and the girls with tearful eyes—a tribute which the poor guide, as he stood trembling with suppressed emotion, did not think it unmanly to bestow also to the sad fate of his fallen companions. After pausing for a time in silence he resumed his narrative by saying,

"Before I attempt to describe the dread scene which was once enacted here, I will go back to the efforts which we made to rescue our imprisoned mates.

"The fire broke out in the morning, soon after the day shift went into the workings, and it was not until six in the evening that we had so subdued the flames that we could send down a dog and a lamp, so as to test the air."

"Excuse me, sir," said Milton, "but why did you send down those things? They could not tell you anything about the air?"

"No, my lad," was the reply; "they could not tell

us anything about the mine; but if the terrible 'black-damp' had been in the shaft, it would have put out the light of the lamp and life of the dog, and that would warn us of the danger of entering it."

"My son," said Mr. Dean, "the element so much dreaded was the same carbonic acid gas which was evolved from the primal globe of fire of which I told you in one of our earliest conversations respecting the formation of the Black Diamond. It is produced by combustion; and then destroys its own parentage when once grown to sufficient power; and as I have told you, the flame of the candle and breath of the dog were but different forms of combustion."

"Thank you, father," was the son's reply; "I think I clearly understand the subject now, and it is exceedingly curious and interesting."

"Well," resumed the miner, "as the dog and candle came up all right, one of the men went down to examine how matters stood, and after a time was drawn up, reporting that he found no difficulty in breathing as far down as he went, which was only halfway, at which point the shaft was obstructed. Two of our brave men went down and removed this, and at about a quarter past seven in the evening reached the foot of the shaft. Venturing up the gangway about sixty feet, they found three dead mules, and then, pressing on, reached the first barricade, which I showed you, when they were compelled to return, very much exhausted by their dangerous explorations. Some time after this, though fully impressed with the fearful risk they would incur, two more of our bravest men—Thomas W. Williams and David Jones—went down the shaft in hope to save some of their comrades, only to be added to the terrible death-list, for they were suffocated before they reached the barrier. But, sir, there were stout-hearted men enough left, even after this sad ending, to go down and secure their bodies, and then no more were allowed to enter the shaft until means had been taken to force fresh air into the mine by constructing a large fan turned by a small engine. It was not until nine o'clock the next morning that all these arrangements were completed, when we felt quite certain that all the poor lads in the pit had perished, and all we could now do was to recover their bodies.

"During the time of erecting the fan a body of more than forty of the bravest and most experienced miners had been formed as a rescuing force. Many times parties descended during the day and up to midnight, but all were compelled to return without accomplishing anything, most of them so completely exhausted that we had to lay them on the grass where they were fanned and nursed by the willing crowd of citizens waiting for developments. It was not until just before the morning of the eighth that two of the dead were found in the mule-stable, and soon after, a large number more were discovered on the east side of the air-way, just before we reached the first barricade. The parties who made these discoveries had to return fearfully under the influence of 'black-damp,' but reported that they had discovered a barrier which they were not able to pass. I came down with the next shift, and helped to tear down the barricade; and when I stepped through and the glare of my lamp fell on the scene, such a sight greeted me as almost made my eyes burst out of their sockets; my hair stood on end, and I became motionless with horror. There lay sixty-three dead men in all possible shapes, with such fearful contortions of limbs and countenances— great staring eyes and open mouths. Oh, sir, it was fearful to behold! There sat Evans, the foreman, on the left hand, leaning forward on his knees, with his mouth open, just as though he was giving an order when the terrible 'damp' snatched his breath away. Just before him one was kneeling, as though engaged in prayer when death arrested his supplication. He was a brave man and a good Christian, and no doubt was praying for his poor fellow-sufferers who had no precious Saviour to comfort them in that dread hour. Fathers were found embracing their sons, and brothers half locked in each other's arms, or with clasped hands, had laid down in their last sleep. All around them were scattered tools, extinguished lamps, dinner-kettles, and cast-off garments, which they had evidently just stripped off for the purpose of stopping the cracks in the barrier, but had fallen dead before they could reach it.

"As soon as we could overcome the shock we began the sad work of getting out the bodies. Nearly all through that dreary day the sad work went on. We would bear the bodies to the foot of the shaft until our platform was loaded with stiffened forms, and then we gave the signal, and they were drawn up to the mouth of the shaft, where another relief of men were waiting to take them away.

"I remained below as long as I possibly could, for I knew what a heartrending scene was transpiring above when these stiffened, blackened forms of fathers, husbands, brothers, and sons were brought into the light and exposed to the gaze of the heart-stricken crowd of weeping wives and mothers and orphan children, who had waited so many hours in agony to behold them. When I did go up, I hardly knew which was weakest, body or mind, for I was kinder stunned by the shocking work in which I had been engaged, as well as half stifled by the poisonous gas."

"I do not wonder at it," was Mr. Dean's remark, "for the whole country was shocked by the sad event, and poured out its sympathy and generosity to mitigate its horrors as far as possible."

"That they did, sir," replied the guide, "and we shall never forget the kindness; but we cannot help remembering that this terrible calamity was in a great measure owing to the criminal neglect of those who sent us down here to work with only one opening through which to escape in case of danger, knowing that an explosion, a fire, or a caving in of the shaft might involve us in certain death. While we, therefore, execrate the name of the miscreant who fired the pit, we cannot altogether withhold our condemnation of those who gave the opportunity to perpetrate the murderous work by such selfish neglect."

"A just sentiment," responded Mr. Dean, "in which an intelligent public fully concurs, and, fortunately for your class, has found expression in the form of legal enactments which, it is hoped, will much lessen the number of calamities in the future."

"For which we miners are most truly grateful," said the guide.

"But now, sir," he continued, "I expect you have

had enough of this sad story, and we will drop the subject, and will, if you please, take a look at the active operations going on in our subterranean world."

"But," said Mr. Dean to his children, while resting for a few moments, "the following incident, taken from a recent number of Good Words, is perhaps one of the most remarkable that has ever occurred, and is no doubt as truthful as it is thrilling:

"In the quiet churchyard of Dailly, within hearing of the gurgle of the Girvan and the sough of the old pines of Dalquharren, lie the unmarked graves of generations of colliers; but among them is one with a tombstone bearing the following inscription:

IN MEMORY OF
JOHN BROWN, COLLIER,
who was enclosed in
Kilgrammie Coal-pit, by a portion of it having fallen in,
Oct. 8th, 1835,
and was taken out alive,
and in full possession of his mental faculties,
but in a very exhausted state,
Oct. 31st,
having been twenty-three days in utter seclusion from the world, and without a particle of food.
He lived for three days after,
having quietly expired on the evening of Nov. 3rd,
Aged 66 years.

"Three weeks without food in the depths of the earth! It seemed hardly credible, and I set myself to gather such recollections as might still remain. I discovered that a narrative of the circumstances had been published shortly after the date of their occurrence; but I was fortunate enough to make the acquaintance of people who were resident in the district during the calamity, and from whom I obtained details which do not seem ever to have found their way into print. Much of my information was derived from an old collier who was one of the survivors. His narrative and that of the other contemporaries of the event brought out in a strong light the superstition of the colliers, and furnished additional evidence as to one of the longest survivals without food of which authentic record exists.

"On the 6th October, 1835, in a remote part of the old coal-mine of Kilgrammie, near Dailly, John Brown, the hero of this tragedy, was at work alone. Sixty-six years of age, but hale in body and full of fun and joke, he had long been a favorite with his fellow-workmen, more especially with the young colliers, whom his humor and his story-telling used to bring to his side when their own term of work was done. Many a time would they take his pick from him, and finish his remaining task, while he sat on the floor of the mine, and gave them his racy chat in return. On the day in question he was apart from the others, at the far end of a roadway. While there an empty wagon came rumbling along the rails and stopped within a foot of the edge of the hole in which his work lay. Had it gone a few inches farther, it would have fallen upon him, and deprived him either of limb or life. There seemed something so thoughtless in such an act that he came up to see which of his fellow-workmen could have been guilty of it. But nobody was there. He shouted along the dark mine, but no sound came back save the echo of his own voice. That evening, when the men had gathered round the village fires, the incident of the wagon was matter of earnest talk. Everybody scorned the imputation of having, even in mere thoughtlessness, risked a life in the pit. Besides, nobody had been in that part of the workings except. Brown himself. He fully acquitted them, having an explanation of his own to account for the movements of the wagon. He had known such things happen before, he said, and was persuaded that it could only be the devil, who seemed much more ready to push along empty hutches, and so endanger men's lives, than to give any miner help in pushing them when full.

"In truth, this story of the wagon came in the end to have a significance little dreamt of at the time.

It proved to have been the first indication of a 'crush' in the pit—that is, a falling in of the roof. The coal-seam was a thick one, and in extracting it massive pillars, some sixteen or seventeen feet broad and forty to fifty feet long, were left to keep the roof up. At first, half of the coal only was taken out, but after some progress had been made the pillars were reduced in size, so as to let a third more of the seam be removed. This, of course, was a delicate operation, since the desire to get as much coal out of the mine as possible led to the risk of paring down the pillars so far as to make them too weak for the enormous weight they had to bear. Such a failure of support led to a 'crush.' The weakened pillars were crushed to fragments, and at the same time the floor of the pit, under the enormous and unequal pressure, was here and there squeezed up even to the roof. Such was the disaster that now befell the coal-pit of Kilgrammie, and it had been the early disturbance of level heralding the final catastrophe which sent the empty wagon along the roadway.

"For a couple of days cracks and grinding noises went on continuously in the pit, the levels of the rails got more and more altered, and though the men remained at work it became hourly more clear that part of the workings would now need to abandoned. At last, on the 8th October, the final crash came suddenly and violently. The huge weight of rock under which the galleries ran settled down solidly on them with a noise and shock which, spreading for a mile or two up and down that quiet vale of the Girvan, were set down at the time as the passing of an earthquake. Over the site of the mine itself the ground was split open into huge rents for a space of several acres, the dam of a pond gave way, and the water rushed off, while the horses at the mouth of the pit took fright, and came scampering, masterless and in terror, into the little village, the inhabitants of which rushed out of doors, and were standing in wonderment as to what had happened.

"But the disasters above ground were only a feeble indication of the terrors underneath. Constant exposure to risk hardens a man against an appreciation of his dangers, and even makes him, it may be, foolhardy. The Kilgrammie colliers had continued their work with reckless disregard of consequences, until at last the cry arose among them that the roof was settling down. First they made a rush to the bottom of the shaft, in hopes of being pulled up by the engine. But by this time the shaft had become involved in the ruin of the roof. A second shaft stood at a little distance, but this too they found to be closed. Every avenue of escape cut off, and amid the hideous groanings and grindings of the sunken ground, the colliers had retreated to a part of the workings where the pillars yet stood firm. Fortunately, one of them remembered an old tunnel, or 'day-level,' running from the mine for more than half a mile to the Brunston Holm, on the banks of the Girvan, and made originally to carry off the underground water. They were starting to find the entrance to this tunnel, when they noticed, for the first time, that John Brown was not among them. Two of the younger men (one of whom had told me the story) started back through the falling part of the workings, and found the old man at his post, working as unconcernedly as if he had been digging potatoes in his own garden. With some difficulty they persuaded him to return with them, and were in the act of hurrying him along, when he remembered that in the haste he had left his jacket behind. In vain they tried to drag him along. 'The jacket was a new one,' he said; 'and as for the pit, he had been at a crush before now, and would win through it this time too.' So, with a spring backward, he tore himself away from them and dived into the darkness of the mine in search of his valued garment. Hardly, however, had he parted from them, when the roof between him and them came down with a crash. They managed to rejoin their comrades; John Brown was sealed up within the mine, most probably, as they thought, crushed to death between the ruins of the roof and floor.

"Those who have ever by any chance peeped into the sombre mouth of the day-level of a coal-pit will realize what the colliers had now to do to make good their escape. The tunnel had been cut simply as a drain; dark water and mud filled it almost to the roof. For more than half a mile they had to walk, or rather to crouch along in a stooping posture, through this conduit, the water often up their shoulders, sometimes, indeed, with barely room for their heads to pass between the surface of the slimy water and the rough roof above. But at length they reached the bright daylight as it streamed over the green holms and autumn woods of the Girvan, no man missing save him whom they had done their best to rescue. They were the first to bring the tidings of their escape to the terrified village.

"No attempt could at first be made to save the poor fellow. As the colliers themselves said, not even a creel, or little coal-basket, could get down the crushed shaft of the pit. The catastrophe happened on a Wednesday, and when Sunday came the parish minister, Dr. Hill—afterward a conspicuous man in the Church of Scotland—made it the subject of a powerful appeal to his people. In the words of a lady who was then and is still resident in the neighborhood, 'he made us feel deeply the horror of knowing that a human being was living beneath our feet, dying a most fearful death. On the Sunday following we met with the conviction that whatever the man's sufferings had been, they were at last over, and that he had been dead some days. On the third Sunday the event had begun to pass away.'

"After the lapse of some days the cracking and groaning of the broken roof had so far abated that it became possible once more to get down into the pit. The first efforts were, of course, directed toward that part of the workings where the body was believed to be lying. But the former roadways were found to be so completely blocked up that no approach to the place could be had save by cutting a new tunnel through the ruins. This proved to be a work of great labor and difficulty; for not only were the materials extremely hard through which the new passage must be cut: a dead body lay in the pit, and awakened all the superstition of the colliers. At times they would work well, but their ears were ever on the alert for strange weird noises, and often would they come rushing out from the working in terror at the unearthly gibberings which ever and anon would go soughing through the mine.

"A fortnight had passed away. The lessee, like the rest of the inhabitants, believed poor Brown to be already dead, and brought a gang of colliers from another part of the county to help in clearing out and reopening his coal-pit. But a party of the men continued at work upon the tunnel that was to lead to the body. They cut through the hard crushed roof a long passage, just wide enough to let a man crawl along it upon his elbows, and at last, early in the morning of the twenty-third day after the accident, they struck through the last part of the ruined mass into the open workings beyond. The rush of foul air from these workings put out their lights, and compelled them to retreat. One of their number was despatched to upper air for a couple of boards, or corn-sieves, or any broad flat thing he could lay hands upon, with which they might advance into the workings, and waft the air out, so as to mix it, and make it more breathable. Some time had to elapse before the messenger could make the circuitous journey, and meanwhile the foulness of the air had probably lessened. When the sieves came one of the miners agreed to advance into the darkness and try to create a current of air; the rest were to follow. In a minute or two, however, he rejoined them, almost speechless with fright. In winnowing the air with his arms, he had struck against a wagon standing on the roadway, and the noise he had made was followed by a distinct groan. A younger member of the gang volunteered to return with him. Advancing as before, the same wagon stopped them as their sieves came against the end of it, and again there rose from out of the darkness of the mine a faint but audible groan. Could it be the poor castaway, or was it only another wile of the arch enemy to lure two colliers more to their fate? Gathering up all the courage that was left in him, one of them broke the awful silence of the place by solemnly demanding, 'If that's your ain groan, John Brown, in the name o' God, gie anither.' They listened, and after the echoes of his voice had ceased they heard another groan, coming apparently from the roadway only a few yards ahead. They crept forward, and found their companion—alive.

"In a few seconds the other colliers, who had been anxiously awaiting the result, were also beside the body of John Brown. They could not see it, for they had not yet resumed their lights; but they could feel that it had the death-like chill of a corpse. Stripping off their jackets and shirts, they lay with their naked backs next to him, trying to restore a little warmth to his hardly living frame. His first words, uttered in a scarcely audible whisper, were, 'Gie me a drink.' Fearful of endangering the life which they had been the means of so marvelously saving, they only complied so far with his wish as to dip the sleeve of a coat in one of the little runnels which were trickling down the walls of the mine, and to moisten his lips with it. He pushed it from him, asking them 'no to mak' a fule o' him.' A little water refreshed him, and then, in the same strangely sepulchral whisper, he said, 'Eh, boys, but ye've been lang o' coming.'

"Word was now sent to the outer world that John Brown had been found, and was yet living. The lessee came down, the doctor was sent for, and preparations were made to have the sufferer taken up to daylight again. And here one of the strangest parts of the story must be told. If by chance the reader has ever been in a coal-pit, he may have remarked that upon the decayed timber props and old wooden boardings an unseemly growth of a white and yellow fungus often takes root, hanging in loathsome tufts and bunches from the sides or roofs wherever the wood is decaying. After being cautiously pushed through the newly-cut passage, John Brown was placed on the lessee's knees on the cage in which they were to be pulled up by the engine. As they rose into daylight, a sight which had only been faintly visible in the feeble lamplight below presented itself, never seen before, and never to be forgotten. That same loathsome fungus had spread over the poor collier's body as it would have done over a rotting log. His beard had grown bristly during his confinement, and all through the hairs this white fungus had taken root. His master, as the approaching daylight made the growth more visible, began to pull off the fungus threads, but (as he told me himself) his hand was pushed aside by John, who asked him, 'Na, noo, wad ye kittle (tickle) me?'

"By nine o'clock on that Friday morning, three-and-twenty days after he had walked out of his cottage for the last time, John Brown was once more resting on his own bed. A more ghastly figure could hardly be pictured. His face had not the pallor of a fainting fit or of death, but wore a strange sallow hue like that of a mummy. His flesh seemed entirely gone—nothing left but the bones under a thin covering of leather-like skin. This was specially marked about his face, where, in spite of the growth of hair, every bone looked as if it were coming through the skin, and his eyes, brightened into unnatural lustre, were sunk far into his skull. The late Dr. Sloan, of Ayr, who visited him, told me that to such a degree was the body wasted that in putting the hand over the pit of the stomach one could distinctly feel the inner surface of the backbone. Every atom of fatty matter in the body seems to have been consumed.

"Light food was sparingly administered, and he appeared to revive, and would insist on being allowed to speak and tell of his experiences in the pit. He had no food with him all the time of his confinement. Once before, when locked up underground by a similar accident, he had drunk the oil from his lamp, and had thereby sickened himself; so that this time, though he had both oil and tobacco with him, he had tasted neither. For some days he was able to walk about in the open, uncrushed part of the mine, where, too, he succeeded in supplying himself with water to drink. But in the end, as he grew weaker and weaker, he had stumbled across the roadway, and fallen into the position in which he was found.

"The trickle of water ran down the mine close to him, and was for a time the only sound he could hear, but he could not reach it. When asked if he had not despaired of ever being restored to the upper air, he assured his questioners that he had never for a moment lost the belief that he would be rescued. He had heard them working toward him, and from the intervals of silence and sound he was able, after a fashion, to measure the passing of time. It would seem, too, that he had been subject either to vivid dreams or to a wandering of the mind when awake, for he thanked again and again the sister of his master for her great kindness in visiting him in the pit and cheering him up as she did.

"On the Sunday afternoon, when some of his old comrades were sitting round the bedside, he turned to them with an anxious, puzzled look, and said, 'Ah, boys, when I win through this, I've a queer story to tell ye.' But that was not to be. His constitution had received such a shake as even its uncommon strength could not overcome. That evening it became only too plain that the apparent recovery of appetite and spirits had been but the last flicker of the lamp of life. Later in the night he died. So strange a tragedy made a deep impression on the people of that sequestered district. Everybody who could made his way into the little cottage to see a man who, as it were, had risen from the dead; and no doubt this natural craving led to an amount of noise and excitement in the room by no means very favorable to the recovery of the sufferer. But this was not all. A new impetus came to the fading superstitions of the colliery population. Not a few of his old work-fellows, though they saw him in bodily presence lying in his own bed and chatting as he used to do, nay, even though they followed him to the grave, refused to believe that what they saw was John Brown's body at all, or at least that it was his soul which animated it. They had seen so many wiles of the devil below ground, and had so often narrowly escaped with their lives from his treachery, that they shrewdly suspected this to be some new snare of his for the purpose of entrapping and carrying off some of their number.

"A post-mortem examination followed, but even that sad evidence of mortality failed to convince some of the more stubbornly superstitious. The late Dr. Sloan, who took part in the examination, told me that after it was over, and when he emerged from the little cottage, a group of old colliers, who had been patiently waiting the result outside, came up to him with the inquiry, 'Doctor, did ye fin' his feet?'

"It certainly had not occurred to him to make any special investigation of the extremities, and he confessed that he had not, though surprised at the oddity of the question. He inquired in turn why they should have wished the feet particularly looked to. A grave shake of the head was the only reply he could get at the time, but he soon found out that had he examined the feet, he would have found them not to be human extremities at all, but bearing that cloven character which Scottish tradition has steadily held to be one of the characteristic and ineffaceable features of the devil, no matter under what disguise he may be pleased to appear.

"And even when the grave had closed over the

wasted remains of the poor sufferer, people were still seeing visions and getting warnings. His ghost haunted the place for a time, until at last the erection of a tombstone by the parishioners with the inscription already quoted, written by the parish minister, slowly brought conviction to the minds of the incredulous. Many a story, however, still lingers, of sights and sounds seen as portents after this sad tragedy. I shall give only one, told to me by an old collier, whose grandmother was a well-known witch, and who himself retained evidently more belief in her powers than he cared to acknowledge in words. Not long after John Brown's death one of the miners returned unexpectedly from his work in the forenoon, and, to the surprise of his wife, appeared in front of their cottage. She was in the habit, unknown to him, of solacing herself in the early part of the day with a bottle of porter. On the occasion in question the bottle stood toasting pleasantly before the fire, when the form of the 'gude-man' came in sight. In a moment she had driven in the cork and thrust the bottle underneath the blankets of the box-bed, when he entered, and, seating himself by the fire, began to light his pipe. In a little while the warmed porter managed to expel the cork and to escape in a series of very ominous gurgles from underneath the clothes. The poor fellow was outside in an instant, crying,

'Anither warning, Meg! rin, rin, the house is fa'ing.' But Meg 'kenn'd what was what fu' brawly," and made for the bed in time to save only the last dregs of her intended potation.

"Most of the actors in the sad story have passed away, and now rest beneath the same green sod which covers the remains of John Brown. With the last generation, too, has died out much of the hereditary superstition. For a railway now runs through the coal-field. Strangers come and settle in the district. An increasing Irish element appears in the population, and thus the old manners and customs are rapidly becoming mere traditions in the place. Even grandsons and great-grandsons of the old women who 'kept the country-side in fear,' affect to hold lightly the powers and doings of their progenitors, though there are still a few who, while seemingly half-ashamed to claim supernatural power for their 'grannies,' gravely assert that the latter had means of finding things out, and, though bedridden, of getting their wishes fulfilled, which to say the least were very inexplicable."

We will not follow the further rambles of the party through the mine, as the scenes afterward witnessed were much the same as those which have been already described in detailing their visits to other mines.

After coming up the shaft and thanking their faithful attendant, who was suitably rewarded, the party returned to Pittston, where Mr. Dean had engaged to spend the Lord's Day, and occupy one of the pulpits to preach to a congregation largely composed of miners and their families. This he did, not only as improving an opportunity to do good, but that his children might see these people under more favorable circumstances than the surroundings incident to their calling.

CHAPTER XIX.

DANGERS OF MINING.

THE tourists enjoyed a delightful day of rest at Pittston. In the morning they attended the Sunday-school before the regular service, and were not a little interested in finding that not only were a large number of the children from the families of the miners, but that many of the teachers were from the same class, being active and intelligent helpers in the good work. At the hour of regular worship Mr. Dean found before him a large and devout congregation, to whom he ministered the word of life, and soon found himself in the warmest Christian sympathy with his hearers, many of whom he recognized as employés in the mines and coal-works which had been visited.

In the afternoon, by special invitation, they attended church, where the service was held entirely in the Welsh language, and Mr. Dean was peculiarly struck with the fervor and devoutness of the worship. Though not understanding the language, there was an unction and spirituality that brought the heart under the sweet influence of the worship, so that the hour was not wholly a gratification of curiosity. On their way back to their hotel, Milton said,

"Well, it's hard to realize that the neat and devout congregation which we've just visited could have been made up of the same blackened and uncouth persons whom we saw in and around the mines, seemingly as stolid and dark in mind as the coal which they were digging out."

"Let the incident, my son," said Mr. Dean, "teach you an important lesson—never to pass judgment on individuals or classes because of the avocation they may be engaged in, if it be an honest one. The employment of a miner necessarily is a disagreeable and dirty one, and deprives him of many opportunities for study and improvement; but, as you see, with less than ordinary advantages he is capable of overcoming these hindrances to advancement, and achieves not only respectability, but distinction. When this is the case, out of whatever class a man may rise, he is worthy of double honor, be it a blacksmith or shoemaker, a tanner or miner."

"I'm sure," remarked Minnie, "that my Sunday among the miners has quite changed my notions about them. Why, some of the girls were as genteel and lady-like as any I ever saw."

"And didn't they sing splendidly?" said Ella; "and one of the best voices was that of the young man whom we met in the shaft the other day, who so politely helped us down the inner tunnel."

"Which same young man, my daughter," remarked the father, "is soon to leave the mine and enter upon a course of study for the Christian ministry, having, in the judgment of his brethren, peculiar gifts for the sacred office. Thus, you see, God chooses his servants now as in the early days of the church, when he called tax-gatherers, fishermen, and charcoal-burners into the ministry. His spirit can go down into the deep mine as well as up into halls of affluence and refinement, and as richly endow the delver after the Black Diamond as he does the most favored sons of those more fortunate ranks of life. As our visits to the mines will make this lesson more emphatic by personal observation, I hope you will hereafter cherish a higher respect, not only for the miner, but for all honest sons of toil, to whom we are so much indebted for the great essentials of life."

When about to resume their ramblings on Monday morning, Milton said to his father,

"I did not quite understand, father, what was said the other day when we were in the Eagle shaft about the fire-damp. I know it is explosive, and that accidents often occur from it; but just how it so differs from the poisonous gases I do not clearly apprehend. Will you please explain the matter a little further?"

"With pleasure, my son. Light carburetted hydrogen gas is colorless and odorless, and about half as heavy as the atmosphere. It is composed of two parts carbon and four of hydrogen, and is the resultant of vegetable decomposition under water or where there is a great deal of moisture; hence it is sometimes called 'marsh-gas,' and by the miners 'firedamp.' Now, coal, being of vegetable origin, and buried deep in the earth, where it is subjected to aqueous influences, gives off great quantities of this gas; and when it cannot find an easy way of escape to the surface, it takes possession of any fissure or cavity in the rocks or coal-seams, and forms a 'blower,' as the miner calls it, such as we saw in the Eagle shaft. The different qualities of coal are dependent on the quantity of this gas present. Starting with the woody fibre, a slight loss of the element forms peat; still more, in conjunction with heat and pressure, lignite; then cannel coal, bituminous coal, and lastly anthracite, whose different qualities are owing to the variation of the gas present; but in all there is much less than in the bituminous coals. From this last quality of coal, illuminating gas is obtained without the addition of any resinous matter; but when anthracite is used, some such substance must be added to supply the lost element. Now, certain influences deprive the bituminous coal-measures of this gaseous property, and they become anthracite; but the carburetted hydrogen, having no way of escape, is kept in the measures in a gaseous state until the miner's drill or pick gives it vent, and it leaps upon its deliverer with fatal impetuosity. The danger from the fire-damp is in the inverse ratio, being greatest in anthracite mines and lessening until the peat is reached, where there ceases to be any cause of fear. This explains why explosions from fire-damp are more numerous in anthracite mines than in the bituminous regions. The manner of these accidents is illustrated when an ignorant person blows out a burner on going to bed or leaving the room. This soon fills the room with gas, and the result is, if a light is taken into it, an explosion immediately follows. This is the precise manner of explosions from fire-damp in mines, only on a scale of much grander proportions. In some pits—as at the Eagle shaft, which we visited, and in West Pittston, where a couple of years ago about twenty men lost their lives—this gas is constantly accumulating from some fissure or the decay of the refuse coal scattered along the damp floors of the gangways and chambers, where it cannot find vent to the surface. Oftentimes when the miner walks along one of these damp passages with no danger from the gas, if he but presses his hand hard upon the floor and places his lamp near the surface, there will be a crackling of sparks, showing that gas is being slowly evolved there. Now, just conceive this pouring out of a stream of fire-damp from one or more blowers, and its slower but constant accumulation from all the damp flowage of the mine, and this for several days in succession, until the whole mine is filled with it; and then a careless miner opens his lamp or makes a stumble, and there follows a flash and a roar in comparison with which the explosion at Petersburg or the powder-ship at Fort Fisher were but as a pop-gun, or as the snap and flash of a Chinese fire-cracker. From chamber to chamber the fiery fiend rushes, and reverberating thunders mark his terrible advent. Flying tramways, falling roofs, shattered pillars, and tumbling shafts are the dire accompaniments, and not unfrequently the lifting up of the entire roof of the mine, which falls back with a universal crush of all below. Then woe be to the poor miners who are beneath it! All that will be left of them will be the torn and shattered limbs, which friends may, perchance, gather up, or which will be left in their deep sepulchre until it is opened at the general resurrection. The Eagle shaft was the scene of one of these explosions, in which seventeen men lost their lives, to be added to the fatal list of the West Pittston disaster. Thus you see that the poor miner works with the agencies of death all around him. The dread poisonous gas settles around his feet, and the fire-damp envelops his head; the one will stop his breath if he stoops, and the other may wrap him in flames if he chances to raise his lamp to look up. Do you understand the subject now, my son?"

"Yes, father, and I certainly pity the poor men who have to earn their living by incurring such fearful risks."

"And they deserve it," replied the father; "but you are not yet fully acquainted with the catalogue of the casualties to which a miner's vocation exposes him. Indeed, terrible as are the fearful results of the noxious gases, they do not equal the more fatal aggregate of deaths occurring from crushing down of roofs, falling rocks and blocks of coal, breaking of machinery, and the thousand and one contingencies that happen to all mining operations.

"The breaking of a beam connected with the pumping engine in the Hartley colliery, situated near New Castle, in England, caused the death of two hundred and four men. When the beam parted, it

fell directly into the shaft, and striking the walls in its descent, tore them down, with all the timbers connected with the machinery, piling up an immense heap of rubbish at a depth of more than four hundred feet from the top of the shaft, too thick and compact to be removed before the poor imprisoned men had all perished. Like the fatal trap at Avondale, the mines had but one entrance, and similar scenes of horror were enacted by the doomed colliers. A large number were crushed beneath the fallen timbers, while a still larger died from inhaling the dread black-damp. When finally opened, it was found that timbers had been cut and repeated attempts made by the poor victims to open the shaft, but all in vain. A half-consumed pony was found near by on which the men had subsisted while struggling for dear life. But when the accident occurred, the ventilating furnaces were in full blast, which soon consumed all the fresh air in the mine, and the men perished by suffocation.

"The history of mining is full of such graphic and terrible visitations, but we will not add to the sad recitals of such tragedies."

It is not necessary that we should follow the tourists in their further exploration among the mines at Pittston. They visited shaft Number Seven, where a severe crush took place, fortunately without the loss of life, caused by a large fall of rain and a spring's thawing. The damage, however, was quite severe; among other things, several dwellings of the miners were precipitated into the vortex. On their way to Scranton several deep basins were pointed out by Mr. Dean, marking similar occurrences; and at Hyde Park they visited the places marked in the town by the sinking of mines which extend under nearly the whole place.

A day was spent at Scranton, much of which was given to the coal-workings in the neighborhood, adding largely to their stores of mining knowledge. From this place the tourists passed to Carbondale, and were particularly interested in watching the tall ventilating shafts, indicated by numerous wooden towers at different points on the way. The old gravity road, similar to the Switchback, also came in for a full share of their attention, especially the grand double planes at Carbondale, up and down which were constant passages of coal-cars. The principal point of attraction, however, was a mine out of which was pumped a stream of water of sufficient volume to have turned a respectable mill. The mine was worked far below the bed of the Lackawanna, which runs near by, and makes an unusually large quantity of water. On visiting the mine, they saw, from the size of its "sump" or reservoir, how easily, from the stoppage of its pumps for any great length of time, it could be inundated. Fortunately, the miners of this country have hitherto been spared any great calamity from this source; but there are cogent reasons for observing all possible care to prevent such an occurrence.

While looking at this new source of danger, Ella said,

"Oh dear! what fearful risks the poor miner does run!—oceans of poison and fire; falling rocks and roofs; breaking of shafts and beams; explosion of fire-damp and gunpowder; and now comes a threatening subterranean deluge! Did any great disaster ever occur from this source, father?"

"Repeatedly, my daughter. Listen, and I will give you one. So late as eighteen hundred and sixty-two, at a mine called Lalle, in France, over a hundred men lost their lives by flooding. Over one part of the mine the river Cèze and one of its tributaries are flowing. On the 16th of October of that year a violent storm visited that part of the country, raising the flood to a higher point than had ever been witnessed before. While the people stood watching the rising deluge, all at once at a certain point a mighty whirlpool was observed as through a seam formed by the outcrop the maddened stream poured with the rush of a cataract into the fated mine below. A cry of horror went up from the multitude, many of whom had husbands and other relatives in the workings, for they well knew the sad fate that had come upon them. Of the hundred and ten men that were in the mine at the time, only five escaped. The mine was converted into a vast subterranean lake, on whose dark surface floated the scores of dead men and horses and the débris of the workings. I know of nothing more thrilling in the struggles for life than the events which led to the rescue of the five men saved. I will quote the graphic description given of these events from L. Simonin's elaborate work on 'Mines and Miners.'

"Whilst a dyke was being made at the surface to keep off the water, and the promptest and surest means of preservation were being studied on the plan, a young rolley-boy, who had previously been employed as a hooker-on in the underground winding, entered into a gallery on Sunday afternoon, the 12th of October, twenty-four hours after the accident took place. He knocked on the walls, and after listening for some time thought he could distinguish sounds answering to his own. Having called his comrades, he repeated the experiment, which was followed by the same result. The engineers were informed; everybody hastened to the spot. M. Parran sent some persons to ensure the utmost silence, and made a signal by knocking with a pick at equal intervals of time, and soon heard, with profound emotion, extremely faint but distinct and timed blows—in a word, the miners' signal—which could not be a repetition of his own.

"A solid wall of more than twenty yards thick intervened between the prisoners and their rescuers, which had first to be cut through, but the greater part of the miners were shut up in the mine. Who would remove the rock? The neighboring companies generously lent their hands, and the first blows of the pick, which were soon heard, bore hope to the hearts of the prisoners. From six o'clock in the evening the work was carried on. Operations were commenced at five different points, by means of inclined drift-ways driven in the direction of the places where the victims were supposed to have taken refuge, the starting-point of these drift-ways being in the very gallery where the signals were heard.

"On Monday, the 14th, at two o'clock in the morning, the captives were communicated with. They said, 'We are three,' and gave their names. The efforts were redoubled, but, as though by a sort of fatality, the coal increased in hardness. Finally, the same day, at midnight, one of the drift-ways reached the hidden place of the prisoners, two of whom were still alive, the youngest sobbing, the other in high state of fever; the third, an old man, was unable to survive the trying ordeal, and lay dead not far from his companions. The most precise details of the circumstances which marked their confinement were taken from the mouths of the rescued colliers. They were at work in a heading when the water was heard coming in upon them, upon which they ran to the upper end of gallery, where they discovered a narrow place with a considerable slope, and very slippery. With their hands and the hook of their lamps they dug a little place in the shaft to sit down in. The water reached to their feet, and they were in a sort of bell, in which the air was highly compressed. They felt a singing noise in their ears, and they lost their voices. Their lamps went out for want of oil. At last they were recovered, after being seventy hours in their close and dark prison, though they thought they had not been in more than half that time."

"Why, father," said Milton, when the sketch was finished, "that was a more terrible disaster than any we have heard of, except Avondale and the Hartley colliery."

"Yes, my son; but the records of mining will reveal more fearful calamities than either of these. The sum total of fatal contingencies in the anthracite regions alone, in eighteen hundred and seventy-one, reached the number of two hundred and seventy-four. This fearful excess marks the additional chances of mortality which the miner has to incur.

"But we will not dwell on this dark, death-side of the picture any longer, as to-day will close our rambles underground, and we must take the sunshine home with us."

"Oh, father," said Ella, "I'm so glad you're through with these terrible scenes, for this last one was so horrid I began to feel as though I could never see anything bright about a miner's life again, and that we ought to stop burning coal."

"Not quite so bad as that, my daughter—every cloud has its silver lining; and though the miner works amid gloom and dampness, exposed to danger and instant death from unusual causes, his life is not spent without many sources of pleasure and refined enjoyment. He has at least remarkable opportunities to study the wonderful handiwork of God as traced out in the formation and uses of the Black Diamond."

"I think," said Minnie, "I should prefer not to be kept quite so long studying one book, and would rather study my lessons in the sunlight than in the dark school-house of the miner."

"That is very natural, my child, and we ought to be devoutly thankful that our lot has been so cast that we can study the ways of God under these more favorable circumstances.

"But now, though our rambles have been so pleasant and profitable, it will be a delightful thought that our further travels will take us nearer home, for to-morrow we shall start in that direction."

"A place which I'm sure," remarked Ella, "I shall appreciate more than ever after wandering through these mining regions, with their black holes staring at us at every turn, and with mountains of coal-dirt over which we must climb."

"Well, perhaps, my children, considered even in that light, our trip may be a paying investment, for whatever binds stronger the home ties is an addition to life's real wealth."

CHAPTER XX.

HOME AGAIN.

AS Mr. Dean on his homeward journey made no further explorations in the mines, the reader need not be delayed with the ordinary incidents of the way, further than to note a day at Pottsville and Port Carbon spent in examinations which added much to their stock of information. This was especially true in reference to the immense traffic in Black Diamonds. Everywhere they noticed the same monster trains coming in from different sections of the coal-regions as they had witnessed with so much wonder at Mauch Chunk. This almost endless stream of coal-trains they followed all the way on their return to Philadelphia, passing an equal number of empty cars on their way back for another load of treasure.

"Only think," said Milton as they were watching this grand succession, "that these immense loads of black stones were once floating in the air, and then passed through the pores of the leaves and built up the great forests that father told us about. It hardly seems as though it could be so."

"And where," asked the father, "are all these black stones, as you call them, now going to, my son?"

"Why, to the cities and towns, of course," was the reply.

"And what then, Milton?"

"They will be burnt up, of course, in our grates and in the furnaces," was the answer.

"And then what becomes of them?" the father still asked.

"What becomes of them? Why, there will be some ashes and cinders left; but the largest part, I suppose, will go into the atmosphere in the form of carbonic acid gas, as you have told us."

"And is it any harder, my son, for the Almighty to take the substance of the coal-measures out of the air than it is to put it back again?"

"Why, no, I suppose not, father," was the son's reply.

"No, my child; God is never perplexed with the processes of nature. He has a storehouse for every element, and a purpose in which to employ it when the time comes to meet the benevolence which he had in view in its creation. The operations of Nature are like a golden chain held in the hands of the great Creator. He binds the links into one grand unity of benevolence, and keeps them bright by constant use. What he locked up by the grand agencies which we have noticed he now unlocks by the same ministry which formed the initial link of the series— fire. The gaseous messenger then set loose, and afterward imprisoned again in the coal-beds, being once more set at liberty, starts on its endless round again, held in the same almighty Hand, and guided by the same divine, benevolent Will. Anon it will take another plunge through leaf and trunk, building up a new growth of vegetation, shorn of its mammoth glory, but subserving a like purpose—to smoulder, perchance, in the pit, transformed into charcoal, or in fire-places, or by the slower process of decay, become a brother to the atmosphere again. Thus the chain is ever moving on its divine mission—God the cause; benevolence the end!"

"It is a grand and beautiful lesson," said Ella, "which I never so clearly and impressively understood as since we began to study the miraculous history of coal, which, at the first, I thought the most unlikely to lead to such results."

"There are, undoubtedly, my daughter, more peculiar and striking facts in the history of coal, and a dramatic element in the processes of removing it from its ancient beds; but all the works of God bear the signet of their divine origin, and he must be dull either of mind or heart who fails to perceive its impress.

"But here is our train, and we must say good-bye to the native treasure-house of the Black Diamond, and seek the waiting, and no doubt anxious, living treasures which we left at Willow Brook."

With this remark the party stepped on board of the cars, and were soon on their winding way back to Philadelphia and home, well satisfied with their week's excursion, during which they had added largely to their treasures of mind and memory.

"There's the dear old home!" shouted Minnie as the familiar willows which shaded the residence of Mr. Dean came into view on the evening of their return.

"Yes," chimed in Milton, "and there's the dearest of mothers waiting at the gate; and won't she get a good hugging soon? And look at old Comfort's gorgeous turban! We shall have a grand reception now, that's certain."

"It will be a hearty and loving one," said Mr. Dean, tenderly; "and we ought to be sincerely grateful for the affection of even the humblest heart, for that is a tribute which even our heavenly Father does not hesitate to earnestly seek after."

"We all, no doubt," said Ella, "will receive a

share in Comfort's appreciation, but I rather suspect that the main stock will be lavished on sister; but don't fear, Min—I'm not at all jealous."

"I'm sure," answered Minnie, "you're all quite welcome to a full share in Comfort's esteem; though I'm not ashamed to own that I love the devoted old creature most tenderly."

The further discussion of this topic was cut short by the stage stopping at the gate of Willow Brook; and the next moment the ardent greetings of the family absorbed every other consideration, in which happy moment the old cook was not overlooked.

When she came to share in Minnie's greetings, she fairly caught the girl up in her arms and folded her to her bosom, while, with joyful tears, she exclaimed,

"Oh, my chile, you'se come back to me! Bres de dear Master who fotch you! I kno's I'se see you agin, for my ole heart follows ye all de way trou' dem dark places, and de bressed Shep'rd, he goes wid ye an' hol's ye up."

"Thank you, dear Comfort," replied the happy girl; "we've had a grand time, and when we get rested I will tell you all about it."

"Bres you, my chile; my ole ears jis hungry to hear ye."

"Well, wife," said Mr. Dean, "you see I have

brought home my charge in tolerably good condition, not requiring very extensive repairs, I hope."

"Yes, husband, I am very happy to have so favorable a report, and you will notice that the house remains on the old foundation yet, though Comfort and I have turned up things somewhat promiscuously in the inside, which, I trust, has led to some improvements rather than to damage."

Mr. Dean looked somewhat inquiringly at Comfort, and said,

"I fear, Comfort, you have not regarded my parting admonition very closely, but have allowed your mistress to overtax her resources of time and strength."

"Now, massa," replied the cook, "you kno's Mis' Liz'beth allus will hab her own way, an' she's done gone an' clean de house from cellar to gar't, an' paint an' whitewash, an' I hab's jes to help her, 'cause de poor chile cou'dn't do it no how hersef."

"Yes, yes, I see, Comfort," replied Mr. Dean; "you both have been rebellious, and very likely you were first in the transgression."

"Truly, husband," said the wife, "if doing nearly all of the work constitutes the greater crime, then Comfort will have to be responsible, for indeed I have had but little hand in it; nevertheless, I assume all the consequences, and will discharge whatever damages may be assessed by disinterested appraisers."

"I see, I see," remarked the husband; "ever since woman was first in the transgression, she has been prolific in excuses for her disobedience, and so I suppose Adam will have to take his bite of the apple, and share the consequences."

"I am very glad," responded the wife, in the same tone of banter, "that you have come home with your gallantry so much improved, for which I will reward you with some supper when you and the children have washed off the dust of travel."

"Which won't take long, dear mother," said Milton, "for I've grown real ravenous since we've been gone, and have just longed for a quiet meal at home."

"Not half so much, my son," said the mother, tenderly, "as I have longed to give it to you."

It is quite needless to detail the animated chat which was held that evening around the tea-table, as each one recounted to the interested mother—every word of which was caught up by the eager and attentive ears of the old cook—the varied impressions and incidents of the week's journeyings. Nor was the stock of wonders exhausted for some time thereafter.

But leaving these things to the imagination of the reader, this sketch of the Black Diamond will find a conclusion in the after-supper conversation of Mr.

Dean, when once more seated in the cosy library so often alluded to in our earlier chapters.

"While the objects which have attracted our attention remain vividly in our minds," said Mr. Dean, "it is best to review our investigations, and see what progress we have made and where we have landed.

"We began with the sublime, initial, self-evident fact that IN THE BEGINNING GOD CREATED THE HEAVENS AND THE EARTH! We have not attempted, as some foolishly have done, to trace the calendar back to its first time-mark, nor, more foolishly still, because unable to do so, have we dethroned the Almighty, and given to blind chance or a soulless evolution the honor and glory of creative power. We found the I AM, not in a burning bush,—though that superhuman phenomenon was such a revelation of the infinite One that the prophet unsandaled his feet and with veiled face bowed in the holy Presence,—but an incandescent world brought us at once into audience with the great Creator, for none other could kindle the universal flame that wrapped the earth in its embraces. Next, amid void and darkness, his presence is brooding over the wild waste of waters, evoking order and dispelling the darkness. Anon life begins its ministry in the deep, and sun and moon to know their appointed times above. As the cycles sweep on, his hand lays the foundations of the mountains, 'being girded with power,' and lifts them up so that the dry land may appear. He fashions the seed, quickens the life-germ, drops it into the earth, and verdure clothes the hills, and drinks up the noxious exhalations of the primal conflagration. It grows until there is a fearful depth of shade, which baffles the efforts of the sunbeam to penetrate it; then the Almighty 'takes up the isles as a very little thing,' and drops them as a covering over the exuberant growth, and thus was laid up the grand stores of Black Diamonds for the coming generations of men who were to bear the image of the great Creator of all things. But the treasure lies buried miles below the surface of the earth, quite beyond all efforts of the puny arm of man to reach it; but God puts his hand beneath its deep foundations, and lifts up the rich gift and drops it within our reach that it may minister to our needs. And shall we, standing with the treasure in our hands, deny the great Almoner either recognition or gratitude? Were all these grand energies subsidized, and the vast epochs of time exhausted simply to put the treasures of creative goodness into our possession, with no expectation of a return, nor design of improvement for a higher purpose still to be wrought out? Such a conclusion would be a gross impeachment of the divine wisdom. It would be to represent all the infinite purposes of God as centred in the gratification of man's animal appetites. Reason and affection would be superfluities, fitful passions, blazing but to die, filling the cup only to make the dregs more bitter. But putting away, as utterly unworthy, this groveling conception, and regarding all the works of God as designed to awaken our minds to thoughts of him, and to fire our hearts with his love, we pass from sense to spirit, we leave the earth and aspire to heaven; we not only act manly, but become God-like, recovering something of that divine image lost by the primal transgression. If we look at nature aright, 'we all, with open face beholding as in a glass the glory of the Lord, are changed into the same image from glory to glory, even as by the Spirit of the Lord.' We only reach the end of God's purpose when we follow the golden chain up to him in whose hand it is held, and then, leaving its links, take hold on God, beyond whom there can be nothing to learn or enjoy.

"Thus we have found in our investigations that, however far back we go, we find Jehovah. 'In the beginning,' with but the faint dawnings of a purpose, the goodness of God called forth an anthem of gladness from the 'sons of God;' and shall we not love and adore him when the wealth of that purpose constitutes the measure of our happiness?

'When all thy mercies, O my God,
   My rising soul surveys,
  Transported with the view, I'm lost
   In wonder, love, and praise!'

"With reason illuminated and with grateful heart, let us look at his purpose as culminating in that bright abode where God is all and in all—an abode to which the redeemed are brought by the atoning grace of our Lord Jesus Christ. 'The same was in the beginning with God. All things were made by him; and without him was not anything made that was made. In him was life; and the life was the light of men.' No one, without this divine illumination, can clearly trace out the beneficent works of God, for somewhere in the process he will be led aside after science falsely so called; and then, though the true light shineth never so brightly, he will not comprehend it, but stumble on, the darkness all the while growing deeper and more dangerous. How much more blessed to have the heart quickened and the ears divinely opened, so that we can hear him say, 'I AM ALPHA AND OMEGA, THE BEGINNING AND THE END'! This bounds all the wondrous mysteries of creation and of grace.

"It would seem that we could hardly choose any object less likely to lead us to such an emphatic and clear recognition of God in the marvels of his handiwork than a lump of dull coal; but our researches have taught us a different and more profitable lesson. All things were made by him, and all things lead to him; and he must be besotted in mind and dull indeed of heart who fails in the recognition of the self-evident fact or stops short of the infinite Presence with an offering of devout thanksgiving.

"Having reached this grand and august finale through the agency of the Black Diamond, we will drop the guide, and

'Crown him Lord of all'

to whom it has led us. But as a memorial of his grace, which not only quickens us with hope, but gives the assurance that, pursuing still the paths which lead us to him, we shall receive a crown of righteousness brighter than the purest diamond ever known among earthly treasures, let us erect as our Ebenezer this massive Black Diamond, and inscribe upon it, as indicative of our gratitude and hope, the light given, and the place reached:

'HITHERTO HATH THE LORD HELPED US!'"

THE END.

www.ingramcontent.com/pod-product-compliance
Lightning Source LLC
Chambersburg PA
CBHW021153230426
43667CB00006B/375